I0099676

Enchantment

Concepts in the Study of Religion

Critical Primers

Series Editor:
K. Merinda Simmons, University of Alabama

Books in the series Concepts in the Study of Religion: Critical Primers offer brief introductions to an array of concepts – modes of analysis, tools, as well as analytic terms themselves – within the discourse of religious studies. Useful for almost any course, the volumes in the series do not attempt to assert normative understandings but rather they introduce and survey the various modes and contexts for scholarly engagement with the concept at hand. How, for example, has the term "myth" been used, and what can various definitions allow us to do as scholars? Who in the field is working on the category of race and how? What might be the future of scholarship on gender in religious studies? What are the possibilities and limitations of description or comparison as methodological approaches? Thus, these critical primers provide – but are not limited to – concise overviews of the history of an approach or term. They also present the authors' own critical analyses of the dynamics and stakes present in discourses surrounding these concepts. Including lists of further readings to guide additional consideration of their topic, the books in this series are valuable resources for students and advanced scholars alike.

The series is published in association with the North American Society for the Study of Religion (NAASR).

Published

Comparison
Aaron W. Hughes

Evil
Kenneth G. MacKendrick

Interpretation
Nathan Eric Dickman

Enchantment

A Critical Primer

Ian Alexander Cuthbertson

equinox

SHEFFIELD UK   BRISTOL CT

Published by Equinox Publishing Ltd.

UK: Office 415, The Workstation, 15 Paternoster Row, Sheffield, South Yorkshire S1 2BX

USA: ISD, 70 Enterprise Drive, Bristol, CT 06010

www.equinoxpub.com

First published 2024

© Ian Alexander Cuthbertson 2024

All rights reserved. No part of this publication may be reproduced or transmitted in any form or by any means, electronic or mechanical, including photocopying, recording or any information storage or retrieval system, without prior permission in writing from the publishers.

British Library Cataloguing-in-Publication Data
A catalogue record for this book is available from the British Library.

Library of Congress Cataloging-in-Publication Data
Names: Cuthbertson, Ian Alexander, author.
Title: Enchantment : a critical primer / Ian Alexander Cuthbertson.
Description: Sheffield, South Yorkshire ; Bristol, CT : Equinox Publishing Ltd, 2024. | Series: Concepts in the study of religion | Includes bibliographical references and index. | Summary: "This book provides an overview of the various ways the concepts enchantment, disenchantment, and re-enchantment have been used both within religious studies scholarship and in related fields. This book will be useful for scholars and students working on a variety of topics including religion in modernity, theories of secularization, conflicts between science and religion, new religious movements, new materialisms, and immanent justifications for environmentalism"—Provided by publisher.
Identifiers: LCCN 2023053418 (print) | LCCN 2023053419 (ebook) | ISBN 9781800504455 (hardback) | ISBN 9781800504462 (paperback) | ISBN 9781800504479 (epdf) | ISBN 9781800505094 (epub)
Subjects: LCSH: Curiosity—Religious aspects—Christianity. | Wonder—Religious aspects—Christianity.
Classification: LCC BF323.C8 C896 2024 (print) | LCC BF323.C8 (ebook) | DDC 155.2—dc23/eng/20240312
LC record available at https://lccn.loc.gov/2023053418
LC ebook record available at https://lccn.loc.gov/2023053419

ISBN–13 978 1 80050 445 5   (hardback)
         978 1 80050 446 2   (paperback)
         978 1 80050 447 9   (ePDF)
         978 1 80050 509 4   (ePub)

Typeset by JS Typesetting Ltd, Porthcawl, Mid Glamorgan

Contents

Acknowledgments

I began to develop some of the ideas that I present in the final two chapters of this book while completing my PhD at Queen's University. During my time at Queen's, I received funding from the Social Science and Humanities Research Council of Canada and from two Senator Frank Carrell Scholarships. I would like to thank James Miller for his valued contributions to my PhD research, and Russell McCutcheon for his support, encouragement, and excellent advice. I am grateful to Jessica McLaren for reading the first draft of this book and providing helpful suggestions and comments and to Joseph Frigault for introducing me to philosophical works on half-belief, for reading sections of this book, and also for all of our many productive conversations over the years. I would like to thank K. Merinda Simmons for her support, encouragement, excellent editorial advice, and for including this book in her series and also the two anonymous reviewers who both provided helpful feedback on this manuscript. Finally, I would like to thank the always enchanting Virginia Noel-Hodge for her extraordinary support and incredible patience.

Introduction

Why Enchantment?

The mark of enchantment ... is that it exceeds all accounts.
Stephen David Ross, *Enchanting*

This book provides a critical introduction to the academic concept "enchantment". Given this focus, it stands to reason that I should begin by defining the term itself. Yet despite the popularity of the term both within and outside the academy, there is no straightforward answer to seemingly simple question: "what is enchantment?" Providing an answer to that question, or rather a series of answers, is my goal in this book. One of enchantment's key features, and one of the main reasons for its slipperiness as an academic term, is that it typically conveys three separate (but often interconnected) ideas. For instance, the *Oxford English Dictionary* defines enchantment as: "1. The action or process of enchanting, or of employing magic or sorcery, and 2. *Figurative*. Alluring or overpowering charm; enraptured condition; (delusive) appearance of beauty." Since the word enchantment is typically used to describe three different things: literal magic, delight, and delusion, the word is necessarily ambiguous. Because the word enchantment is an integral component of two key academic terms – disenchantment and re-enchantment – this ambiguity has repercussions.

Although the earliest recorded use of enchantment in its literal sense in the *OED* dates to 1297, enchantment's status as an academic concept – or as an integral component of an academic concept – is much more recent. Max Weber, one of the founding figures of modern sociology, famously alluded to enchantment in his lecture *Science as a Vocation*, which he delivered in 1917. Yet Weber's lecture does not actually include the word enchantment. Rather than explicitly discuss enchantment, Weber describes instead *the disenchantment of the* world. Or, rather, this is how his German term *Die Entzauberung der Welt* is typically translated into English.[1] Yet the English word disenchantment is not a perfect match for the German word *Entzauberung*. First, the root of the German word is magic (*zauber*) and not enchantment. Second, as Jason Ānanda Josephson-Storm has argued, the German *Entzauberung* signals something that is in process rather than a completed action (Josephson-Storm 2017). Strictly speaking, therefore, Weber does not describe the disenchantment of the world but rather the "demagicking" of the world. Despite these translation issues, Weber is routinely described as the first *scholar* to employ the term disenchantment in the way it is most often used in contemporary English language scholarship. As I explain more fully in the next chapter, with few exceptions, disenchantment is commonly used today to describe an intellectual preference for scientific and technical explanations over magical ones, along with an associated loss of meaning and wonder.

Disenchantment is an important concept in religious studies scholarship. Since Weber first coined the term, disenchantment has been used as a key descriptor of modernity, as an important feature in accounts of secularization, and as a way of distinguishing between pre-modern and modern religious forms. Modernity is often described as involving a radical shift from previous modes of living in, organizing, and interpreting the world, and disenchantment is often presented as both an important cause and as a major effect of this shift. Scholarly accounts of secularization, or the apparent decline of religious belief and practice in modernity, also depend on the notion of disenchantment – so much so, in fact, that the two terms are sometimes viewed as being synonymous. While accounts of secularization describe the apparent decline of religious belief and practice in different ways, disenchantment, or the modern preference for rational and scientific explanations, is typically viewed as a

---

1. Weber's term *Die Entzauberung der Welt* actually appears in print for the first time in his 1913 article *Über einige Katergorien der verstehenden Soziologie* or *Some Categories of Interpretive Sociology*; yet scholars most often cite Weber's use of the term in *Science as a Vocation* when describing disenchantment (Josephson-Storm 2021).

major driver of secularization. Although secularization has recently become a somewhat "unfashionable theory", it continues to influence scholarship in religious studies along with work in related subfields such as nonreligion (Bruce 2011). Finally, Weber developed the term disenchantment in order to describe modern processes of rationalization and intellectualization that, in his view, had important repercussions for religious belief and practice (Weber 1958, 2020). For Weber, disenchantment involved not only preferring scientific explanations over religious ones but also important changes within religions themselves. Weber described increased rationalization within religion, and especially within Calvinist Protestantism, as a variety of disenchantment according to which "magical" beliefs and practices are increasingly discarded.

While disenchantment is a key concept in religious studies, it is not limited to that field alone. Disenchantment has also been used by critical theorists, most notably Max Horkheimer and Theodor Adorno, to describe modernity's deleterious effects. For Horkheimer and Adorno, the modern disenchantment of the world helps to produce exploitative capitalism, deceptive mass culture, totalitarianism, and fascism, each of which ultimately leads to human enslavement and subjugation. Disenchantment has also been used as a term in arguments concerning the place of religious justifications in legal proceedings. According to the legal scholar Steven D. Smith, secular discourse has become disenchanted such that individuals must conceal supernatural bases for their beliefs or arguments – a situation that, in his view, renders public discourse shallow and superficial. I consider both these approaches to disenchantment in later chapters.

Like disenchantment, re-enchantment is also a key term both in religious studies and in other fields. While some scholars argue that disenchantment never happened, others argue that although disenchantment did take place, the world is increasingly becoming re-enchanted. Pointing to the growth of various new religious movements and alternative spiritualities, scholars have argued that modern individuals are increasingly rejecting cold scientific rationality in favour of magical beliefs and practices. Other scholars have argued that re-enchantment involves fully secular (i.e. non-religious) strategies for creating wonder and delight in an otherwise rational and disenchanted world. These scholars often focus on fictional literature and other cultural artefacts as sources of modern re-enchantment. Natural sites have also been described as important sources of wonder, delight, and enchantment. Some scholars argue that returning to premodern animistic conceptions of nature will re-enchant the natural world, motivate environmentalism, and thereby help mitigate climate change and prevent further ecological disasters.[2] Others point instead to human interactions with the natural world and especially with animals as productive sites of both re-enchantment and ecological consciousness.

Even though "enchantment" has increasingly been used as an academic term in its own right in recent years – especially as an immanent justification for environmentalist projects and in recent work related to the field of new materialism, which I discuss in Chapter 4 – it most often appears embedded in the terms disenchantment or re-enchantment. As a scholarly concept, discussions of enchantment itself are eclipsed by accounts of its apparent disappearance or reappearance. In fact, enchantment is seldom the focal point in academic accounts and is revealed instead in the negative space created by the figures of disenchantment and re-enchantment. So, why write a book about enchantment? If disenchantment and re-enchantment are the more commonly used terms, why not write a book about one or both of them instead? The issue, as I see it, is that while there are many books that explore disenchantment or re-enchantment, because these terms describe enchantment's disappearance or reappearance, their meaning necessarily depends on that which has apparently disappeared or returned. Importantly, scholarly descriptions of disenchantment and re-enchantment employ the three different meanings of "enchantment" (magic, delight, delusion) in different ways and for different purposes. By focusing on "enchantment" itself, I am better able to distinguish between the various ways both disenchantment and re-enchantment are used in contemporary scholarship.

---

2. The term animism refers to the idea that various non-human beings including animals, plants, and natural features (e.g. mountains, rivers) possess souls or spirits and therefore deserve moral consideration.

For some scholars, disenchantment primarily entails the disappearance of *belief* in magic, spirits, and invisible forces, while for others it entails changes in the way humans *feel* about the world. Depending on how enchantment is imagined, disenchantment can signify a largely negative development (less delight and wonder), a positive one (less delusion), or an ambivalent combination of the two. Likewise, scholars who describe re-enchantment use that term in very different ways. Scholars who view enchantment as involving belief in magic and spirits and associated behaviours describe re-enchantment as involving a revival of magical thinking and practice. Those who see enchantment primarily in terms of positive emotions describe the return of delight and wonder free from any magical associations. Scholars who focus on all three meanings of enchantment describe instead a variety of rational re-enchantment that is explicitly free from both delusion and superstition.

Although this book is about enchantment, because enchantment is at the centre of both disenchantment and re-enchantment, this book is as much about these concepts as enchantment itself. I have three main goals in exploring how the concept enchantment is variously deployed both on its own and also as a component of disenchantment and re-enchantment. First, I present, in a single volume and to my knowledge for the first time, a concise and critical overview of all three concepts. Second, I provide some conceptual clarity, for I suspect that many of the disagreements concerning whether disenchantment or re-enchantment have taken place stem from the fact that each of these terms is used to mean very different things depending on which variety of enchantment is thought to be disappearing or reappearing. Although many academic concepts are ambiguous, enchantment's three very different connotations make it especially worthy of disambiguation. Third, I propose a new approach to enchantment that rejects the common binary distinction between both enchantment and disenchantment and between disenchantment and re-enchantment. This approach highlights instead how modern individuals may be productively and playfully both enchanted and disenchanted at the same time or, in my terminology, fluidly enchanted.

Chapter Summaries

Chapter 1: The Disenchantment Thesis

In this chapter, I provide an overview of the disenchantment thesis. Popularized by Max Weber, the disenchantment thesis argues that specific modern developments have caused irreversible intellectual and affective changes such that modern individuals prefer scientific explanations over magical ones and are increasingly immune to feelings of fullness, mystery, and awe. Because disenchantment is often described both as an important feature of modernity and as involving important changes to religious belief and practice, I begin the chapter with a brief overview of modernity and secularization. I then provide overviews of the three most well-developed arguments for disenchantment: Max Weber's arguments concerning intellectualization and rationalization, Charles Taylor's account of a shift from what he calls porous to buffered selves, and Marcel Gauchet's description of increased transcendence and the modern shift away from sacral dependence.

Chapter 2: Disenchantment as Modern Myth

In this chapter, I consider empirical evidence both for modern disenchantment and for premodern enchantment in an attempt to determine whether disenchantment provides an accurate account of historical changes or whether it is, as some scholars claim, merely an influential but ultimately misleading modern myth. I begin by noting that Max Weber, Charles Taylor, and Marcel Gauchet all fail to provide sufficient evidence to support their claims that the premodern world was enchanted in the first place. I then briefly examine textual and archaeological evidence for premodern magical beliefs and practices and consider whether the available evidence is sufficient to support the specific claims concerning disenchantment put forward by each scholar. Next, I consider whether available empirical evidence supports the claim that enchanted beliefs and practices have actually disappeared in the modern world. Drawing on recent surveys, I argue that global levels of belief in magic, spirits, and invisible forces cast doubt on whether disenchantment has, in fact, taken place. Finally, I consider to what extent modern religious forms really are less magical than premodern ones in an attempt to determine whether or not religion has in fact become disenchanted as Weber, Taylor, and Gauchet claim.

Chapter 3: Enchantment and Exclusion

In this chapter, I describe how enchantment and related terms including magic and superstition have been and continue to be used as markers of difference that exclude particular individuals and groups in various ways. I trace a brief history of the terms magic and superstition in order to show how these common descriptors of enchantment have been used to mark particular beliefs and practices as unacceptable, dangerous, and as worthy of exclusion. First, I outline how both terms were used within religious discourse to exclude unacceptable beliefs and practices. Next, I explore how the meaning of each shifted after the Enlightenment such that both magic and superstition became markers of credulity, faulty reasoning, and intellectual inferiority rather than religious unacceptability. Finally, I show how discourse surrounding magic, superstition, and by extension enchantment works to exclude particular groups and individuals including religious individuals, indigenous persons, people of colour, women, and children from the standard model of modern, intelligent, and rational human beings.

Chapter 4: Rational Re-enchantment

In this chapter, I describe a particular version of re-enchantment in which enchantment primarily involves heightened emotions or affective states and in which re-enchantment therefore involves delight that is free from the delusion associated with premodern belief in magic and spirits. I begin with an overview of the theoretical framework that supports this view of re-enchantment, focusing primarily on the work of Michael Saler and Jane Bennett. I also outline some arguments for secular re-enchantment put forward by a number of scholars working in different fields. Borrowing from Jane Bennett's description of the various potential sources of enchantment, I organize these accounts of secular re-enchantment into three general categories: culture, technology, and nature. For each category, I provide a brief outline of the specific variety of disenchantment that is apparently being reversed by rational re-enchantment.

Chapter 5: Spiritual Re-enchantment

In this chapter, I describe a different version of re-enchantment, one in which enchantment pertains to interactions with magic, spirits, and invisible forces and re-enchantment involves the recovery of pagan belief and practice or else the creation of new alternative spiritual paths. I begin by outlining the most detailed theoretical account of spiritual re-enchantment, focussing on the work of Christopher Partridge and his description of occulture. I describe a variety of "neo-pagan" new religious movements in which many practitioners both believe in and actively engage with gods, magic, and spirits. Next, I consider a range of popular alternative spiritual beliefs and practices that focus on contact with spirit entities and alternative healing practices and which are often categorized as "New Age". Finally, I explore the renewed interest in the presence of ghosts and spirits in modern society along with individuals who claim to be able to communicate or interact with them.

Chapter 6: Modern Enchantment

In this chapter, I describe my own take on enchantment. I draw upon the theoretical frameworks discussed in previous chapters along with recent philosophical work on the connections and disjunctions between belief and behaviour to propose a novel approach to an understudied variety of modern enchantment – a variety that I refer to as "fluid enchantment". I begin by outlining the binary model of belief on which the accounts of enchantment, disenchantment, and re-enchantment rely. Next, I outline three accounts of partial belief that challenge the binary model. Finally, I outline the ways the concept fluid enchantment might be used to describe situations and contexts in which individuals partially, ironically, or playfully engage with magical or supernatural beliefs and practices without fully adhering to these beliefs and without necessarily viewing these practices as being straightforwardly effective.

Conclusion: The Future of Enchantment

I conclude the book by considering how the concept enchantment might best be deployed in future scholarship. I begin by outlining recent arguments that the term enchantment should be divested of its religious or supernatural connotations and reimagined to refer uniquely to heightened emotions or affective states. I argue that ignoring the ways "enchantment" has been associated with supernatural beliefs and practices impoverishes our ability to accurately describe modern engagement with posited spirits and invisible forces. I then argue that, to the extent enchantment signifies the playful attitude described in Chapter 6, it may provide a productive space for thinking, believing, and experiencing things otherwise.

Chapter 1

The Disenchantment Thesis

The world is big enough for us. No ghosts need apply.
Sherlock Holmes in Arthur Conan Doyle,
"The Adventure of the Sussex Vampire"

According to proponents of the disenchantment thesis, human understanding, experience, and behaviour have changed in drastic and potentially irreversible ways over the last few centuries. In its standard form, the disenchantment thesis argues that, whereas humans used to understand and experience the world as being inhabited by a variety of supernatural agents (spirits, ghosts, god(s), demons) and as being filled with a variety of powerful invisible forces (magic, fate), this is simply no longer the case. From the perspective of disenchantment, whereas value and mystery once permeated human beings' lived realities today we live in a world devoid of mystery – a world that can, at least in principle, be mastered through scientific calculation.

Descriptions of the precise *nature* of disenchantment, the specific *causes* that precipitated disenchantment, and the particular *effects* that disenchantment entails for human experience vary in important ways. There is, in other words, no single disenchantment thesis. Scholars have conceptualized the apparent changes that disenchantment involves in different ways and so there are instead several connected disenchantment theses. I write "apparent changes" because, as I explain in the next chapter, many scholars take issue with the standard account of disenchantment as a whole or else dismiss particular claims raised by proponents of disenchantment.

In this chapter, I outline some of the most well-developed and influential arguments for disenchantment, focusing on the work of Max Weber, Marcel Gauchet, and Charles Taylor. However, in order to explore what disenchantment means for each of these scholars and also more generally, it is necessary first to trace the contours of two key concepts that are closely connected to and are essential for understanding disenchantment: modernity and secularization.

Modernity

For most proponents of the disenchantment thesis, disenchantment is a symptom or else a component of a larger constellation of intellectual, social, political, economic, and demographic changes that tend to be associated with "modernity". Modernity, like all academic concepts, has been interpreted and described in various ways. As Bruno Latour writes in his book *We Have Never Been Modern* (1993), "[m]odernity comes in as many versions as there are thinkers ..." (10). As is the case with disenchantment, scholars not only disagree about the specific changes that modernity entails but also disagree concerning when, to what extent, and even whether these changes did (or did not) take place. Despite these important points of contention, modernity is a generally coherent and hugely influential concept.

The term modernity is often used to mark a temporal distinction. Sometimes, the word is simply used to describe the present moment. However, modernity generally indicates present or recent times as distinguished from the remote past. Like other temporal designations, modernity describes not only the inevitable passage of time but also important changes in the organization of human life. What makes modernity modern, therefore, is its proximity to the here and now, as well as its important differences from premodern (or traditional) ways of life. For this reason, the onset of modernity tends to be associated with specific developments in Western society, culture, and intellectual life that began during the late Medieval period and that culminated in the twentieth century. Some key developments associated with modernity include: an increase in **rational and scientific thought**, often associated with the Enlightenment and Scientific Revolution, which challenged revealed religious truths or customary knowledge; **industrialization**, which entails the use of machinery and standardized production processes in place of human or animal labour; the growth of **capitalism** as an economic system, which involves market exchange, the reinvestment of profits for growth, and wage labour; **urbanization**, or the growth of cities and the movement of populations from rural to urban areas; **secularization**, which I explore in greater detail below, but which involves an overall decline in the influence and practice of religion in society; and finally, **disenchantment** (Giddens and Sutton 2021: 11, 78). Given the sheer number of important changes outlined above, modernity is often viewed as having created a dramatic and definitive break with traditional or pre-modern society. In Peter Berger's evocative terms, modernity constituted a "cataclysmic and unprecedented event in human history" (1979: 2).

Taken together, these developments affected not only the organization of society (new industries, larger cities, different economic relations) but also the ways human beings interact with and make sense of the world and each other. As S.N. Eisenstadt notes, "the core of modernity is the crystallization and development of a mode or modes of interpretation of the world ..." (2000: 321). One such mode of interpretation involves a new orientation toward time that can be encapsulated by the notion of *progress* (Chakrabarty 2002: xix). From the perspective of progress, the differences between modern and non-modern societies outlined above are not neutral but instead constitute improvements or advancements. From this perspective, the past becomes something to overcome or leave behind, a "heap of ruins", pieces of which might be used to build a new and better future (Theborn 2003: 294).

Another mode of interpretation involves a new orientation toward knowledge and truth according to which scientific knowledge takes precedence over all other forms of knowledge, especially those connected to religion and tradition. As Stephen Gaukroger notes, the "self-image" of modernity involves "the gradual assimilation of all cognitive values to scientific ones" (2005: 1). Likewise, in *Modernity: Understanding the Present*. Peter Wagner describes modernity as the belief in the human capacity to reason and the view that the world is fundamentally intelligible or amenable to human intelligence (2012: 4). One potential consequence of this shift involves a kind of flattening of human experience. Writing in 1903, Georg Simmel described the modern mind as becoming "more and more calculating" and as developing a "matter-of-fact attitude" which leads to a blasé attitude or sense of indifference. For Simmel, modern indifference causes objects to appear in "an evenly flat and grey tone", which means that "no one object deserves preference over any other" (Simmel 1997: 177–178). As I explain below, the idea that modernity instils a preference for scientific knowledge that results in a flattening of human experience and increased indifference or detachment is a key feature of both the disenchantment and secularization theses.

The term modernity has been extensively criticized. Scholars have noted that many descriptions of modernity reveal a Eurocentric bias and take for granted that modernity was first and foremost a product of European civilization, even if modern changes were later imposed or adopted elsewhere (Eisenstadt 2000; Asad 2003). If progress is a key component of modernity, then non-modern societies or groups must be "backward" and in need of development or improvement. Indeed, modernity and associated programmes for development and modernization have been and continue to be used to justify colonialism and imperialism. In this view, concepts like modernization are wielded as "political weapons" (Martin 2014: 467). For critics of the concept modernity, distinctions between modern and non-modern societies are never neutral but instead produce value-laden binaries: modern societies are seen as developed, rational, civilized, and emancipated, while non-modern or traditional societies are seen instead as undeveloped, irrational, uncivilized, suppressed and are therefore in need of development or civilizing (Diabzar et al. 2013: 646). As I explain in Chapter 3, the concept "disenchantment" has been analysed and criticized in similar ways.

Secularization

Like disenchantment, secularization is often seen as an important feature or consequence of modernity. Yet while both disenchantment and secularization have been used to describe the fate of religious ideas and practices in the modern world, secularization and disenchantment differ in significant ways. Whereas secularization tends to be used to describe an overall decrease in the influence and presence of religion in modernity, disenchantment typically describes a societal or individual preference for specific modalities of thought and experience.

The English term "secularization" – along with secular, secularism, and secularity – derives from the Latin word *saeculum*. Originally, *saeculum* referred to a large expanse of time, but the word took on specific religious connotations when Christian writers used it to distinguish between ordinary time, which can be measured and understood in human terms and "higher" time associated with God and eternity. Eventually, the term "secular" was used to differentiate between regular clergy who live apart from the mundane world in monasteries and secular clergy who act and live "in the world". It also distinguished between religious authorities (e.g. bishops) and non-religious or lay authorities (Taylor 2007). Today, the word secular more broadly evokes a straightforward binary distinction between religion and not-religion – a binary that has been amply criticized in recent decades (see McCutcheon 1997; Arnal and McCutcheon 2013; Cuthbertson 2018a). The term secularization, then, refers to a process by which something becomes less or no longer religious. Sometimes, the term is used to describe a particular historical event, such as the seizure of church property by the state, but more often the term refers to a variety of modern developments that have caused religion either to decline in the modern world or else to change in significant ways. Put simply, secularization proposes that "modernization causes problems for religion" (Bruce 2002: 2).

Although scholars disagree as to the precise problems secularization causes, most accounts of secularization agree that differentiation, pluralization, privatization, and rationalization are among the most important modern secularizing developments (Jakobsen and Pellegrini 2008). **Differentiation** can involve a separation between particular social spheres (religious vs. secular, private vs. public) but also between the social functions served by specific institutions. For instance, whereas the institution of the Medieval Catholic Church once fulfilled many different functions in society such as providing education and health care, functional differentiation entails the creation of separate (non-religious) institutions such as government-run schools and hospitals (Bruce 2011). **Pluralization** involves instead the multiplication of religious and non-religious explanations and ideas in society and an associated decrease in the taken-for-granted nature of traditional explanations. Proponents of pluralization as a secularizing modern development argue that because pre-modern societies were largely homogeneous and enjoyed high levels of social cohesion, traditional (religious) views were highly plausible. The increase of competing views made possible by new modern transportation and communication technologies reduced the plausibility of traditional religious views along with their importance as explanatory frameworks (Berger 1979). **Privatization** describes processes according to which religion is contained within particular institutions or contexts or else becomes a thoroughly individual private concern. Scholars who focus on privatization describe the marginalization of religion: whereas religion once structured society as a whole, its relegation to specific religious institutions (churches) or to individual conscience (beliefs) caused a decrease in religion's social influence (Casanova 1994). Finally, **rationalization** refers to an overall increase in instrumental cause-and-effect thinking that is often linked to the increased value placed upon scientific outlooks and approaches in modernity (Wilson 1982). Although it remains unclear whether or to what extent science and religion are actually opposed to one another, the notion that scientific knowledge threatens religious outlooks is widespread.

Proponents of secularization argue that the modern changes secularization entails decrease religion's social significance (differentiation and privatization), lessen the plausibility of religious views (pluralization and rationalization), and result therefore in an overall decrease in religious participation or "the displacement of religion from the centre of human life" (Bruce 2011: 1). Like modernity and disenchantment, secularization has also been extensively criticized. Critics of the secularization thesis have questioned both the empirical basis for secularization, along with the ways accounts of secularization support particular ideological and political goals.

From the empirical standpoint, scholars have argued that the pre-modern past was not as religious as is commonly assumed. For instance, in his article "Secularization RIP", Rodney Stark argues that religious belief and practice were perhaps less prevalent and widespread in Medieval Europe than is usually thought (Stark 1999). Likewise, while rates of religious belief and participation may have declined in Western Europe, religious belief and practice remain prevalent in the United States and elsewhere (Torpey 2012). Even former proponents of secularization have revised their earlier claims in light of new empirical evidence. Peter Berger has argued both that the secularization thesis has been "empirically falsified" and that the modern world remains "intensely religious" (Berger 2012: 313). Yet despite evidence that religion continues to enjoy prominence globally, proponents of secularization have argued that this constitutes de-privatization rather than a challenge to secularization as a whole (Casanova 1994) or that regardless of high levels of global religious affiliation, individual commitment to religion has nevertheless declined (Bruce 2011).

From the political and ideological standpoint, critics have claimed that although secularization has been presented as a value-neutral claim about the fate of religion in the modern world, secularization is tied to "ideological notions of the direction of history and the teleology of progress ..." (Martin 2014: 464). In other words, secularization's descriptive enterprise is also a normative one. From this perspective, secularization, like modernity, is tied to notions of "higher" (i.e. secular) civilizational forms and the apparent persistence of religion in particular (often non-Western) locations is stigmatized and presented as "backward" (Göle 2010). Precisely because secularization and "the secular" are such value-laden terms, there are potential costs associated with maintaining religious affiliation and belief in modernity; or as Sara Mahmood puts it, "one cannot inhabit the label 'nonsecular' indifferently in our age but must bear the consequences of such an inhabitation" (Mahmood 2010: 294 n19).

Disenchantment 1: Max Weber and Rationalization

On 7 November 1917, Max Weber (1864–1920), a German political scientist and one of the fathers of modern sociology, delivered a lecture to a group of students at Munich University entitled "Wissenschaft als Beruf" (commonly translated into English as "Science as a Vocation").

In this lecture, Weber famously described *Die Entzauberung der Welt*, or the disenchantment of the world. The root of the German word *Entzauberung* is *zauber* (magic) and so *Die Entzauberung der Welt* is sometimes translated instead as "the de-magicking of the world". Since Weber coined the phrase, the disenchantment of the world has been discussed, theorized, and criticized in hundreds of academic manuscripts and in thousands of academic articles.[1] Indeed, although Weber's concept of disenchantment has been interpreted and applied in varying ways, the term has become key to understanding modernity and the place of religion in the modern world.

In "Science as a Vocation", Weber focuses on the work of scholars and considers the value and meaning of scholarship and teaching. While Weber's remarks on scholarship remain insightful, the most famous and oft quoted passage occurs near the middle of the lecture when he describes the disenchantment of the world. Weber introduces the concept of disenchantment while describing two other processes: rationalization and intellectualization. According to Weber, intellectualization and rationalization cause disenchantment. He argues that both intellectualization and rationalization are consequences of technological advances but notes that neither term is synonymous with advanced technology nor indeed with an overall increase in knowledge:

> Increasing rationalization and intellectualization does *not*, in other words, mean a greater knowledge of the conditions we live under. Rather, it means something else: the knowledge, or belief, that we *could* find out if we *wanted* to; that in principle there are no mysterious or incalculable forces intervening in our lives, but instead all things, in theory, can be *mastered* through *calculation*. It means the disenchantment of the world. Unlike the savage for whom such mysterious forces existed, we no longer need to adopt magical means to control or pray to the spirits – we make use, instead, of technology and calculation.
>
> (Weber 2020: 17, italics in original)

---

1. The phrase "the disenchantment of the world" is sometimes attributed to the German playwright and philosopher Friedrich Schiller (1759–1805). However, while Schiller described the de-divinization of nature (*Die entgötterte Natur*) in his poem *The Gods of Greece*, Schiller did not describe disenchantment as such.

For Weber, disenchantment involves a particular attitude toward knowledge itself. According to this disenchanted attitude, the world and everything in it is fundamentally knowable. Importantly, Weber does not claim that scientific advances will necessarily produce final certain knowledge nor that humans will eventually know everything that can be known. From the perspective of disenchantment, although certain facts may be ultimately unknowable, this is always only ever the result of practical limitations rather than being a consequence of some inherent or unavoidable mysteriousness. According to this view, whereas humans once knew or believed that some features of the world were fundamentally mysterious and were therefore impossible to either fully understand or to explain, the attitude of epistemological confidence that disenchantment provides – the confidence that all knowledge is attainable – removes all such mystery from the world.

Weber argues that humans have been subject to the processes of intellectualization and rationalization "for thousands of years" (ibid.). For him, intellectualization refers broadly to the development of abstract thought and of careful analysis, especially of texts (Weber 1963: 253). According to Weber, the process of intellectualization produces an intellectual class that is unhindered by everyday practical concerns and is therefore able to occupy itself with the systematization of knowledge for its own sake (ibid.: 102). Specialized work in philosophy and in scientific fields are, for Weber, products of intellectualization.

Rationalization refers to a wider range of processes and developments in Weber's work. Although rationalization is sometimes described as involving an increase in means-ends thinking and a growing concern with practical efficiency (Giddens and Sutton 2021: 21), because Weber uses the term "rational" in several different ways, rationalization can also refer to describe several different developments. Depending on the type of rationalization at work, the concept can mean practical efficiency, adherence to a set value or system of values, the systematization of ideas, or acting according to set formal rules.

Weber uses the term "purposive rationality", also sometimes called practical rationality, to describe means-ends thinking according to which a person achieves her specific idiosyncratic objectives (ends) by interacting with people or objects in the world (means) (Weber 2019: 101). An increase in means-ends practical thinking would therefore constitute purposive or practical rationalization. An individual who becomes increasingly goal-oriented and efficient in achieving her goals would undergo a process of purposive rationalization.

Weber distinguishes purposive rationality from "value rationality". Whereas a course of action is purposively rational if a particular goal is achieved through efficient means, a course of action is value rational if that action aligns instead with a system of values, no matter the outcome (ibid.). A value rational action is one that is consistent with a particular value, even if that action fails to achieve any goal and is therefore purposively or practically irrational. For Weber, particular values are never rational or irrational in themselves. Because human beings hold different values, a given action (e.g. being brutally honest) can be value rational for someone who values honesty while being value irrational for someone who values kindness.

Weber uses the term "theoretical rationality" to describe instead a type of rationality that is directed toward abstract thought and the systematization of ideas. Whereas both purposive rationality and value rationality are concerned with specific actions, theoretical rationality refers instead to theorization for its own sake. The careful elaboration of some field of knowledge would be theoretically rational, therefore, even this systematization was carried out without any practical goal in mind and without any appeal to values and so was both purposive and value irrational.

Finally, Weber also describes "formal rationality" as a means-end calculation that is structured not by idiosyncratic goals and efficient means (purposive rationality) but rather with reference to rules, laws, or regulations (Kalberg 1980: 1158). Any action that is directed by bureaucratic rules (e.g. applying for a passport) or that follows a set formal procedure (as with the scientific method) would be theoretical rational in Weber's framework.

Rationalization therefore suggests more than simply preferring the practical calculation of efficient means-ends thinking over the magical means that pre-modern individuals apparently preferred. As Weber puts it, "rationalizations of the most varied character have existed in various departments of life and in all areas of culture" (Weber 1958: 26). Importantly, rationalization is not necessarily a linear or irreversible process; instead, "multifaceted rationalization processes recurrently surfaced and then faded away amidst a tapestry of shifting balances and kaleidoscopic interweavings" (Kalberg 1980: 1172–1173). For instance, while Weber describes the overall trajectory of religious belief and practice in terms of rationalization, he also describes the religious prioritization of otherworldly (spiritual) goals over this-worldly (practical) goals as a variety of "irrationalization" (Weber 1963: 27). Likewise, rationalization does not necessarily entail the elimination of religious belief or of magical thought or behaviour. As Weber explains, both religious and magical behaviours are often concerned with achieving practical results in the world, which means that from the standpoint of purposive rationality, "religiously or magically motivated behaviour is relatively rational behaviour ..." (ibid.: 1).

For Weber, rationalization does not cause religion to disappear or to lose its social significance (secularization) but instead creates *new varieties* of religious belief and practice. Weber argues that the development of a coherent pantheon in Greek and Roman religion, in which gods acquired specific attributes and differentiated responsibilities, is the result of theoretical rationalization (ibid.: 10). Likewise, the development of set protocols for worship and rules for daily living in Judaism were, for Weber, the products of rationalization as well (ibid.: 13). Finally, in *The Protestant Ethic and the Spirit of Capitalism*, Weber famously argued that rationalization led to the development of an "inner-worldly asceticism" especially within Calvinist Protestantism. He linked this particular ethical rationality with the development of capitalism as both an economic system and a system of values (Weber 1958).

Given his claims concerning the basic rationality of both religion and magic, it seems clear that neither religion nor magic are irrational as such for Weber. As Josephson-Storm has argued, processes of rationalization are perhaps destined to rationalize rather than erase magic in modernity by creating a separate "magic sphere" in which magical professionals pursue practical ends (purposive rationality), adhere to set values (value rationality), theorize magical means (theoretical rationality), or produce bureaucratic systems (formal rationality) for the management of their profession (Josephson-Storm 2021). While Weber does connect both rationalization and disenchantment to "the elimination of magic from the world", Weber is perhaps not describing an empirically verifiable fact but rather an intellectual shift, itself the result of various forms of rationalization, that caused magic to be repudiated as mere superstition (Weber 1958: 105). This repudiation of magic, which culminated within Christianity in the disavowal of perceived "superstitious" and "magical" elements of Medieval Catholicism during the Protestant Reformation and also in the reconfiguration of Catholic practice in the Counter Reformation, occurred in a particular context and was driven by specific goals and values.

Yet while disenchantment, for Weber, entails an intellectual shift away from magical means rather than the literal de-magicking of the world, this intellectual shift nevertheless has associated real-world effects. One such effect involves a shift in the location of values in the modern world. As Weber puts it in *Science as a Vocation:*

> It is the destiny of our age: given the rationalization and intellectualization of the times, and especially given the disenchantment of the world – its loss of magic – the ultimate and most sublime values have retreated from public life, into either the otherworldly realm of mysticism or the direct brotherly communities of individuals with one another.
>
> (Weber 2020: 40)

Whereas public life was once structured by taken-for-granted value systems, given processes of rationalization, such obvious and unquestioned value systems can exist only in limited domains. In modernity, public life is structured by multiple competing value systems and this forces individuals to choose from among various value postulates resulting in a situation that Weber describes as the *polytheism of values* (ibid.: 30–31). The modern preference for scientific explanations also sets limits on the kinds of things that are worth knowing or are possible to know. Weber wonders whether anyone actually believes that scientific fields such as biology, physics, or chemistry can produce knowledge about the *meaning* of the world and claims instead that science serves primarily "to uproot and destroy the belief that the world has *any such thing* as a 'meaning'" (ibid.: 22, italics in original).

Weber also links the rationalization, disenchantment, and focus on salvation that Calvinism promoted with a particular orientation to beauty and emotion. Weber associates disenchantment with "a fundamental antagonism to sensuous culture of all kinds" (1958: 105) and rationalized Protestantism with the "rejection of everything that is ethically irrational, aesthetic, or dependent upon [...] emotional reactions to the world ..." (1963: 168). In the final pages of *The Protestant Ethic and the Spirit of Capitalism*, Weber describes the rationalized and disenchanted modern world as bound by the technological and economic conditions of machine production and as fixated on acquisition and efficiency. For Weber, these conditions cause humans to become enclosed in a shell as hard as steel or imprisoned in an iron cage (1958: 181). As was the case with Georg Simmel's assessment that modernization causes a detached blasé attitude, disenchantment in Weber's framework carries possible negative experiential or affective consequences as well. Although Weber leaves open the possibility that "new prophets" may arise or that there may be "a great rebirth of old ideas and ideals", he also describes the iron cage of disenchantment as involving "mechanized petrification" and "nullity" (ibid. 182).

Disenchantment 2: Charles Taylor and Immanence

Ninety years after Max Weber coined the term disenchantment, the Canadian philosopher Charles Taylor (b. 1931) published his influential book *A Secular Age*. Like Weber, Taylor is interested in theorizing modernity and exploring the ways modern individuals understand and experience the world. In *A Secular Age*, Taylor is particularly interested in diagnosing the fate of religion in modernity in response to what he calls a modern shift toward "secularity". For Taylor, secularity is not synonymous with secularization. Whereas secularization describes a decline in religious belief and participation along with a reduction in religion's influence in society, Taylor's term secularity introduces a third dimension: important changes in the *conditions of belief* in the modern world. In Taylor's framework, these changes in the conditions of belief constitute disenchantment.

Given Taylor's focus on modern changes, it is important to understand precisely what modernity means for him:

> By *modernity* I mean the historically unprecedented amalgam of new practices and institutional forms (science, technology, industrial production, urbanization), of new ways of living (individualism, secularization, instrumental rationality), and of new forms of malaise (alienation, meaninglessness, a sense of impending social dissolution).
>
> (Taylor 2002: 91)

These new practices, institutional forms, ways of living, and varieties of malaise are in some ways universal in that any society that earns the designation "modern" will exhibit some broad mixture of these new developments. However, in *A Secular Age*, Taylor is particularly interested in modernity as it developed in the West or, more precisely, the "North Atlantic World" (Taylor 2007: 1). For Taylor, the developments listed above coupled with the growth of a radically secular public sphere have created an *immanent frame*, one that structures the lived conditions of individuals and society in the modern West (ibid.: 192, 543). The concept of an immanent frame depends upon a binary distinction between immanence and transcendence. In Taylor's usage, transcendence refers broadly to the idea that meaning and value exists *beyond* human life (in god(s), the cosmos) while immanence refers instead to the idea that meaning and value exist only *within* human life and concerns (ibid.: 15). The movement from a transcendent frame to an immanent one in modern Western society depends, in part, upon an increase in secularity.

Taylor breaks down his larger concept of secularity into three varieties, which he straightforwardly labels secularity 1 (S1), secularity 2 (S2), and secularity 3 (S3). S1 refers to the overall retreat of religion in public life or to what I described as the processes of privatization and differentiation. S2 refers instead to the decline of religious belief and practice. S3 refers more broadly to changes in the conditions of belief or the shift according to which religious belief is no longer axiomatic or taken-for-granted in society. As Taylor puts it, the shift to S3 involves "a move from a society where belief in God is unchallenged and indeed, unproblematic, to one in which it is understood to be one option among others, and frequently not the easiest to embrace" (ibid.: 3). While S1 and S2 constitute important modern changes, Taylor is most interested in exploring the conditions of belief in modern Western secular society (S3).

Taylor uses the term disenchantment to encapsulate the changed conditions of belief he describes. For Taylor, as for Weber, disenchantment is not synonymous with a decline of religious beliefs or practices. Like Weber, Taylor notes that disenchantment is, in fact, a key feature of particular religious forms, especially those of Protestantism and post-Reformation Catholicism (ibid.: 553). Taylor describes disenchantment as involving the replacement of what he calls enchanted "porous selves" with disenchanted "buffered" ones. As these adjectives suggest, a porous self is one that is open to (or vulnerable to) outside influences, whereas a buffered self is instead closed to (or protected from) these influences. What links porous selves with enchantment (and buffered selves with disenchantment) is the nature of these outside influences. For Taylor, these influences are otherworldly and include god(s), spirits, and moral forces. For a porous self, god(s), spirits, and both magical and moral forces straightforwardly exist and also act or impinge upon human life. But being porous in this sense is not merely a matter of *believing* in the existence of god(s), spirits, or otherworldly forces but concerns instead the ways individuals *experience* the world (ibid.: 39). There is an important difference, in other words, between merely believing that God exists or that magic is real and living in a world in which God or magic is a basic and obvious "fact" of our lived experience.

The shift from a porous self to a buffered one involves a shift in the location of both agency and meaning. For a porous self, while agency and meaning reside in humans they also reside *outside* the human realm: invisible forces are capable of acting upon human beings and god(s) or moral forces that exist beyond the human realm are capable of providing meaning to human life. For a buffered self, both agency and meaning *only ever* reside in minds and especially in human minds. As a result, "the buffered self begins to find the idea of spirits, moral forces, causal powers with a purposive bent close to incomprehensible" (ibid.: 539). Again, this shift in the location of agency and meaning involves more than a shift in belief or theory. For a buffered self, it is axiomatic that agency and meaning exist only in human minds. The obvious reality of this fact forms an integral and unavoidable feature of that person's lived experience of the world. For Taylor, the buffered self is a key component of the immanent frame.

This shift in the location of both agency and meaning has important effects for what Taylor refers to as "fullness". For Taylor, fullness describes any activity or condition in which "life is fuller, richer, deeper, more worthwhile, more admirable, more what it should be" (ibid.: 5). This fullness also evokes a sense of wonder and an investment in those aspects of the world or the cosmos that transcend mundane concerns (Warner et al. 2010: 12). Disenchantment, or the replacement of porous selves with buffered ones, dissolves the notion that there are higher levels of being that humans can aspire to and also the experience of having the world respond in some real sense to human interests. In place of a responsive cosmos, disenchantment provides a mechanistic universe that is unresponsive and indifferent to human concerns (Taylor 2007: 280). In other words, the immanent frame carries its own malaises of immanence which include a sense that meaning is both fragile and arbitrary, as well as a recognition of the utter flatness and emptiness of ordinary life (ibid.: 309). Bereft of enchantment, modern buffered selves exist in an endless and unavoidable crisis of meaning. Although buffered selves are no longer vulnerable to unwanted influences from god(s), spirits, magic, or moral forces, they are also invulnerable or closed off from meaning and significance (ibid.: 303). As with Weber, Taylor's disenchantment carries specific negative experiential and affective consequences. From Taylor's perspective disenchantment leads to the loss of something that is beneficial (fullness) and the acquisition of something that problematic (flatness).

Disenchantment 3: Marcel Gauchet and Transcendence

In 1985, Marcel Gauchet (b. 1946), a French historian and philosopher, published *Le Désenchantement du Monde: Une Histoire Politique de la Religion* which was later translated into English as *The Disenchantment of the World: A Political History of Religion*. In his book, Gauchet considers how developments in the ways humans think about god(s), society, political organization, and themselves led to important changes in the nature and structure of both religion and society. For Gauchet, the disenchantment of the world involves the expulsion of invisible forces from our conceptions of nature, which leads inexorably to the "impoverishment of the reign of the invisible" in human life and society (1997: 3).

Although Gauchet accepts that science and technology contribute to disenchantment as he describes it, he also argues the expulsion of invisible forces is, paradoxically, the consequence of an increased focus on transcendence within religions themselves. For Gauchet, disenchantment relies on a distinction between the immanent here and now and a transcendent realm beyond this world. Like Weber and Taylor, Gauchet identifies modernity as a key engine of disenchantment. For Gauchet, modernity involves the development of representational politics, a systematic investment in the future, knowledge based on objective causes, efforts to control and manage nature, and viewing increased material productivity as an end in itself (ibid.: 103). But modernity also entails what Gauchet describes as a "rupture in being"[2] according to which the "here-below" (*l'ici-bas*) and "the beyond" (*l'au-delà*) no longer constitute a single unified entity (2004: 114). In defining modernity in terms of rupture, Gauchet posits a distant past in which these two orders or reality (the immanent visible here-below and the transcendent invisible beyond) were once unified.

For Gauchet, this basic unity is the defining feature both of "primeval religion", by which he means religions that existed before 1000 BCE, and also of "primitive religions" that continue to exist in societies with no formal State apparatus. Unlike some earlier scholars of religion who employed evolutionary frameworks and thus viewed later religious forms as more developed or advanced, Gauchet describes primeval religion instead as "religion's most complete and systematic form" (1997: 23). For Gauchet, the "primordial essence of the religious" involves two key features: sacral dependence and customary

---

2. All translations from the French are my own.

permanence (ibid.: 28). **Sacral dependence** refers to the idea that primeval and primitive religion alike are structured with reference to otherworldly beings (gods, ancestors). According to Gauchet, the driving force behind human action, customs, and meaning in primeval and primitive religion is not human thought or agency but rather a received framework associated with "totally different beings, whose difference and sacrality lies in the fact that they were creators ..." (ibid.). From this perspective, the entirety of human existence depends upon a sacred source in primeval and primitive religions; in primeval and primitive contexts, therefore, religion and society are practically coextensive. **Customary permanence** describes the logical consequence of sacral dependence: if human existence depends upon a sacred and therefore inaccessible source, then the structures of primeval and primitive societies must be static and permanent. Because human existence along with the structure and customs of primeval and primitive societies depend upon a posited sacred realm, it is meaningless to distinguish between the here-below and the beyond. In primeval society, the visible here-below – the everyday world and its rules and customs – are for Gauchet completely determined by a sacred and invisible beyond. As Gauchet explains, in primeval and primitive societies "the visible and invisible are entwined in a single world" (ibid.: 31).

The first cracks in the primeval unity Gauchet describes begin to appear alongside the eventual development of political coercion or force, which he connects to the State. Gauchet links the development of political force with the arrival of rulers who begin to reorganize society, its customs, and its laws with reference to sacred beings. By claiming to represent the will of sacred beings, rulers become intermediaries between human beings and god(s). As a result, the sacred basis for society becomes increasingly visible and accessible through its intermediaries. For Gauchet, the coercion that rulers enact in the name of god(s) replaces formerly unquestioned (and unquestionable) sacral dependence with social structures that are increasingly socially questionable (ibid.: 36). More importantly, the figure of a ruler who is able to communicate with and act upon the will of sacred beings creates a decisive split between the here-below and the beyond. Although human existence continues to be structured with reference to an invisible sacred realm, the presence of intermediaries signifies this realm is distinct from rather than practically coextensive with human society. The immanent world remains linked to the transcendent one, but it becomes a mirror image reflected through the policies and actions of its rulers. For Gauchet, this first crack in primeval unity eventually creates a permanent split between the immanent and transcendent realms – one that has important consequences for religion and the former "reign of the invisible". As Gauchet puts it, "political domination, which decisively entangles the gods in history, will prove to be the invisible hoist lifting us out of the religious" (ibid.: 37).

According to Gauchet, this distancing of the invisible transcendent realm from the visible immanent one results in a major shift in the nature of religious experience and in human beings' understanding of the world. Gauchet argues that the logical conclusion of this distancing is the idea of a personified version of the transcendent realm in the form of an omniscient and fully transcendent God. This idea of a single transcendent God creates important repercussions for religious experience: whereas the structure of religion and society had once been nearly synonymous with an inaccessible sacred realm, religion and society become increasingly shaped by the will of a single transcendent being with whom humans can communicate. For Gauchet, this shift leads to an increase in speculative thinking. If God's will can be communicated, then the ultimate foundation of the world is at least partly accessible to human reason, and humans are therefore compelled to question and to form beliefs about God's plans. In other words, whereas religion once shaped human society as a whole, it now becomes increasingly a matter of individual experience and belief (ibid.: 101). This religious affirmation of transcendence, the complete separation of God from creation and the self-sufficiency of the created world is, for Gauchet, "at the heart of the modern revolution in the conditions for knowledge" (ibid.: 53). Humans not only seek to understand divine will but also begin to view the world as being intelligible independent of God. This modern revolution is the basis for both increased theoretical rationality and for the development of objective scientific knowledge (Gauchet 2004: 115).

Increased transcendence also leads to a shift in the source of human meaning. Given an increase in speculative thinking, Gauchet argues that humans begin to develop a sense of inwardness and begin to rely on their own beliefs and interpretations as guides for their actions. This inwardness results in existential angst: humans are compelled to ask unanswerable questions concerning the meaning of the world and their place inside it. As Gauchet puts it, "[f]rom now on we are destined to live openly and in the anguish from which the gods had spared us ... each of us must work out our own responses" (1997: 207). In part, this angst also derives from an inability to understand fully the invisible realm in modernity. For Gauchet, human beings cannot avoid postulating an invisible beyond or being fascinated by its mystery. The difference between modern humans and our ancestors is not a lack of interest in the beyond but rather an inability to satisfy that interest or to fill in the disturbing gap that transcendence creates (Gauchet 2004: 162–163). As was the case with Weber and Taylor, for Gauchet disenchantment creates negative consequences.

The Disenchantment of the World focuses primarily on the consequences of religious developments. Although Gauchet describes a "post-religious" world, the world created by increased transcendence is not without religion. For Gauchet, religion does not disappear in modernity but rather radically changes its form, becoming a matter of individual belief rather than a synonym for social structure. Yet Gauchet also considers the fate of magical beliefs in modernity. Much in the same way that disenchantment does not entail the disappearance of religion or the human interest in "the invisible", neither does it result in the disappearance of magical thinking. In fact, he argues that magic persists even after transcendence has unfolded to its full extent (1997: 46). Just as Gauchet describes humans as inevitably being fascinated with the invisible realm, he also notes "there is a certain mystical/magical view of things that is inherent in our thought and which is by no means destined to disappear" (2004: 162). But while Gauchet describes the "indestructible survival" of magical thinking and the "invincible tendency" to understand reality with reference to "invisible influences", he also explains that modern magical thinking is most often undertaken in a "cautious mode" of the "well, you never know ..." variety (ibid.: 151). As was the case with religious belief, modern humans submit magic to rational scrutiny. In other words, while horoscopes and séances may persist in modernity, their persistence is not evidence of the "failure of desiccating scientism" (ibid.). For Gauchet, while the world may be objectively disenchanted, it will nevertheless appear as subjectively enchanted to those individuals who engage in magical thinking and practices (ibid.: 162).

Conclusion

The term disenchantment has been used to describe several different developments in the modern world. For Weber, disenchantment describes an intellectual preference for rational means over magical ones and an associated antagonism to aesthetic and emotional reality. In Taylor's view, disenchantment involves a shift in modern conditions of belief according to which the existence of god(s), spirits, and unseen forces loses its taken-for-granted status. It also involves the development of buffered selves for whom it becomes axiomatic that all meaning derives from immanent human minds rather than from transcendent sources. Both these developments result in an associated loss of fullness. For Gauchet, disenchantment is instead a revolution in religious thought according to which God becomes increasingly transcendent; religion becomes associated with individual belief rather than societal structure; and humans face unavoidable existential angst while remaining fascinated with an unknowable invisible realm and engaging cautiously in magical thinking. Despite their differences, what each view of disenchantment has in common is a posited pre-modern world that is different from the modern world in important ways: a pre-modern world that was, in other words, *enchanted*.

Each description of disenchantment alludes to a pre-modern enchanted world that was challenged or restructured by specific modern developments. But given the differences between the disenchantment theses described above, each of these posited pre-modern enchanted worlds is in some ways unique. For Weber, the pre-modern enchanted world is fundamentally and unavoidably mysterious;

rather than rely on rationalized science, humans attempt to master or implore a variety of spirits. For Taylor, whose view of disenchantment is closest to Weber's, the pre-modern enchanted world is one in which the existence of god(s), spirits, and invisible forces is taken for granted, in which meaning has a transcendent source, and in which humans are able to experience fullness. According to Gauchet's take on disenchantment, the pre-modern enchanted world is instead one in which the transcendent and immanent realms are unified, in which religion and society are synonymous, and in which humans are free from existential angst.

In order to determine whether or how well each disenchantment thesis accurately describes the modern changes it posits, it is necessary to consider both whether the pre-modern world to which each thesis alludes really was enchanted and also whether the particular disenchanting modern changes each thesis describes have actually taken place. I turn to these questions in the next chapter.

Chapter 2

Disenchantment as Modern Myth

The single most familiar story in the history of science is the tale of disenchantment – of magic's exit from the henceforth law governed world. I am here to tell you that as a broad cultural history, this narrative is wrong.

Jason Ānanda Josephson-Storm, *The Myth of Disenchantment*

The standard form of the disenchantment thesis outlined in the preceding chapter – the idea that modernity has stripped the world of supernatural agents and forces, that modern humans prefer rational and scientific explanations over magical ones, and that this affects how humans understand and experience the world – can be challenged along two empirical axes. First, the alleged enchanted nature of premodernity can be called into question. For unless the premodern world was one in which humans really did take the presence and power of invisible forces and magical means for granted, the apparent absence of such forces and means in modernity would constitute a continuation of the status quo rather than disenchantment. Second, the alleged disenchanted nature of modernity can be called into question. For if invisible forces, magical means, and other enchantments persist in modern society, the modern world cannot be meaningfully described as *dis*enchanted. If the premodern world was not enchanted and the modern world has not become disenchanted, then the disenchantment thesis is merely a powerful, immensely popular, but ultimately misleading narrative: it is both a modern myth and one of the central myths of modernity. In this chapter, I consider whether the premodern world really was enchanted; whether the modern world is, in fact, disenchanted; and whether or not religion has become disenchanted in modernity. I begin by examining the empirical evidence for premodern enchantment.

Premodern Enchantment

Each of the three disenchantment theses outlined in the first chapter posits an enchanted premodern world that is radically different from an apparently disenchanted modern one. Before considering the empirical evidence for premodern enchantment and modern disenchantment more broadly, it is worth examining the evidence, or lack thereof, provided by Weber, Taylor, and Gauchet in support of their theses. Problematically, while each scholar claims the premodern world is enchanted in various ways, these claims are seldom supported with actual evidence.

For Max Weber, Calvinist Protestantism is the "logical conclusion" of the "great historical process in the development of religions" according to which magic is eliminated from the world (Weber 1958: 105). Yet according to Robert W. Scribner, because Weber's interpretation of Protestantism focuses primarily on the theological writings of key reformers, it ignores the ways in which magic persisted as a central concern in popular Protestantism and in the everyday practices of Protestant lay persons and clergy alike (1993). Despite Protestantism's official dismissal of "Catholic magic", for instance, images of Martin Luther were believed to "provide magical protection" well into the eighteenth century (Bailey 2007: 198). Likewise, while Weber asserts "mysterious forces" existed for "the savage" in *Science as a Vocation*, he fails to provide any historical evidence whatsoever to support this assertion. Instead, Weber takes it for granted that mysterious forces existed for "primitive" or premodern individuals without actually demonstrating whether, why, or to what extent this was the case.

Similarly, Charles Taylor asserts "everyone can agree that one of the big differences between us and our ancestors of five hundred years ago is that they lived in an 'enchanted' world and we do not ..." (Taylor 2010: 302). Yet as Jon Butler notes, Taylor does not provide any historical evidence to support his claim that the average premodern individual was somehow porous and therefore more open to posited supernatural influences (Butler 2010: 201). While Taylor admits that, short of returning with a time machine and handing out questionnaires, it may be impossible to determine whether the majority of premodern individuals really did believe in supernatural influences, he nevertheless argues that common seemingly magical practices such a ringing bells for protection from storms indicate such beliefs were prevalent (Taylor 2010: 315). Given Taylor's focus on the lived experience of premodern individuals in comparison to modern ones, however, it remains unclear to what extent specific practices actually reveal the inner experience of their practitioners. According to Taylor's logic concerning church bells and storms, the mere practice of my reading (or not reading) my horoscope in the daily newspaper would indicate whether or not my lived experience includes the posited invisible influence of celestial objects. However, as I explain in the final chapter, it seems likely that outward behaviours do not perfectly reflect inner reality but are instead produced by experiences, beliefs, and emotions in complex and sometimes contradictory ways.

Likewise, while Gauchet posits a premodern world in which invisible forces once reigned and in which society was shaped by a sacred and invisible beyond, Gauchet's claims concerning premodernity are also entirely unsupported by historical evidence. Indeed, in defining primeval religion as that which occurs prior to political coercion in the form of the State, Gauchet describes a variety of religion that existed prior to historical records and about which there can be no real historical evidence. While archaeological evidence does exist pertaining to the practices of prehistoric humans, determining whether such evidence actually supports Gauchet's claims is difficult. Further, Gauchet does not refer to any such archaeological evidence in support of his claims concerning primeval religion. He does consider "remnants of societies existing prior to the state" (Gauchet 1997: 23) as providing evidence for what primeval religion must have been like in prehistory, but it remains unclear whether or why contemporary "primitive" societies would possess a religious outlook that is identical to that of prehistoric humans.

Although evidence for beliefs and practices that might plausibly earn the designation "enchanted" or "magical" is largely absent from the most well-developed scholarly accounts of disenchantment explored in the first chapter, evidence for magic is nevertheless present in the historical record. Indeed, scholarly accounts of magic in the premodern world provide numerous examples of apparently enchanted beliefs and practices. In his book *Magic in the Middle Ages*, Richard Kieckhefer describes the fifteenth century *Munich Manual of Demonic Magic*, which "gives instructions for conjuring demons with magic circles and other devices, commanding the spirits once they have appeared, or compelling them to return after they have been dismissed" (2014: 6). Kieckhefer also describes archaeological evidence for magical amulets and papyri discovered in Egypt and which were dated to the fourth and fifth centuries CE along with numerous texts from Greek, Roman, and Egyptian antiquity concerning the magical properties of animals, stones, and plants and the influence of celestial bodies (ibid.: 29–40). Likewise, in his book *Enchanted Europe: Superstition, Reason, and Religion, 1250-1750*, Euan Cameron draws on a wealth of theological writing on various superstitions to describe sorcery, enchanted weapons, magical cures for various ailments, rites for exorcising agricultural pests, and various forms of divination (Cameron 2010). In addition to archaeological and theological evidence, fictional literature and mythology from Homer's *Odyssey* and Shakespeare's *A Midsummer Night's Dream* to Norse Sagas and Celtic literature also abound with magical figures and themes. Given both the archaeological and textual evidence for premodern magic, it is certainly possible that the average premodern individual really did experience the world as enchanted. As Keith Thomas puts it in his book *Religion and the Decline of Magic*, it may be the case that while "astrology, witchcraft, magical healing, divination, ancient prophesies, ghosts and fairies are now all rightly disdained by intelligent persons ... they were taken seriously by equally intelligent persons in the past ..." (Thomas 1971: ix).

Although archaeological and textual sources provide evidence that premodern individuals seemingly engaged with and certainly wrote profusely about magic and other enchantments, it remains less clear whether such evidence can be used to determine either the extent to which magic was a feature of the lived reality of premodern individuals or the extent to which premodern individuals felt themselves to be "porous" in the face of invisible forces and powers. While magic and enchantment certainly seem to be prevalent in premodern texts, not all such references to magic betray an unproblematic belief in its efficacy. Much in the same way that some writers in antiquity were sceptical of religion, others were in turn sceptical of the efficacy of magic and other enchantments. Cicero (106 BCE–43 BCE), for instance, ridiculed the popular idea that dreams could be used as a source of divination. Similarly, while numerous magical texts such as the *Munich Manual* existed in fifteenth-century Europe, not all of the magic described in these texts was accepted as efficacious or plausible. Marginal notes in a book of household management from Wolfsthurn Castle describe one magical cure for menstrual problems as "utterly false, superstitious, and practically heretical" (quoted in Kieckhefer 2014: 5).

Using Christian theological texts to trace the contours of premodern magic in Europe is also problematic. Because theologians produce normative texts or texts that describe how Christians should (or should not) practice Christianity, these texts provide "the very opposite of neutral, disengaged description" (Cameron 2010: 9). It remains unclear, therefore, to what extent the extant theological literature on magic or superstition describes practices that might have been a part of the lived reality of premodern humans (ibid.: 8). Using fictional literature to trace the contours of the lived reality of premodern humans is even more problematic. For if the mere presence of magical elements in a given society's fictional accounts reveals the extent to which its members assume magic to exist or for invisible forces to impinge upon them, modern Western society would, by that measure, be thoroughly enchanted.

The enchanted premodern world posited by Weber, Taylor, and Gauchet differs from the modern one not only in terms of the supposed presence of magic and other enchantments but also in terms of human emotion or experience. For Weber, whereas the modern disenchanted world is one that encloses us in a shell as hard as steel or imprisons us an iron cage, the enchanted premodern world was one in which life was structured by taken-for-granted value systems and in which individuals were able to find reliable sources of meaning. For Taylor, the disenchanted modern world is flat, empty, and devoid of higher purpose, whereas in enchanted premodernity individuals inhabited a responsive cosmos that generated its own sense of fullness. According to Gauchet, disenchanted modernity creates unavoidable existential angst, while our premodern ancestors were spared from such troublesome existential questions. As was the case when considering whether magic constituted an unproblematic component of the lived experience of premodern humans, determining whether premodern individuals were really able to reliably encounter meaning, experience fullness, or avoid existential angst in their daily lives is a complicated task. Today we have access to a wealth of sociological data on human happiness and fullness, but no such data exist concerning premodern humans. As a result, anyone interested in attempting to understand the emotional lives of premodern humans must turn to written documents in their attempt to imagine the emotional and psychological lived reality of premodern life.

Yet even a cursory exploration of written records from premodernity casts doubt on the claim that the lived experience of premodern humans was somehow replete with meaning and fullness while being free from existential angst. Medical texts from antiquity, for instance, describe melancholia as a common physiological and psychological affliction that results in lengthy bouts of inexplicable fear, sadness, and anxiety (Bell 2014); ancient philosophers carefully considered what fulfilment means as well as how best to achieve it, which seems to indicate fulfilment was by no means a given in antiquity; autobiographical works such as Augustine of Hippo's *Confessions* and Peter Abelard's *The Story of my Misfortunes* reveal the complex challenges and doubts each writer faced; and literature from Sophocles' *Oedipus Rex* to Shakespeare's *Hamlet* describe instances of existential angst. Nor is it clear that the presence of magic and other enchantments in premodernity necessarily coincide with greater fullness or a lack of existential angst: historical texts that describe premodern magical spells and formulae indicate such magic was often used to increase fullness (e.g. love charms) and to mitigate the dangers inherent in human existence (birth, illness, death). Although modern humans certainly face uniquely modern problems, it seems reasonable to assume that a lack of fullness and existential angst are problems faced by all humans – even premodern ones. Arguably, the diagnoses of both premodernity and modernity that Weber, Taylor, and Gauchet put forward tell us more about their own values and hopes than they do about either premodernity or modernity.

Modern Enchantment

Most appraisals of modernity and modern progress frame the modern world as increasingly rational and disenchanted. From this perspective, magical beliefs and practices along with beliefs in spirits, ghosts, and other supernatural entities should be practically absent in our scientifically advanced and thoroughly modern world. Yet despite scholarly accounts of modernity as rational and disenchanted, recent survey results indicate that many modern humans believe in the kinds of invisible powers, mysterious forces, and supernatural agents that are typically associated with our supposedly enchanted premodern past.

Astrology

Broadly speaking, astrology maintains that events on earth and human character traits are determined to some extent by the movements and relative positions of celestial bodies. If the modern world really is disenchanted, then belief in the invisible influence of the planets should no longer exist. Yet, as anyone who reads newspapers or magazines can attest, astrological horoscopes are commonplace. In the United States, many of the largest daily newspapers publish horoscopes including the *Washington Post*, the *LA Times*, the *Tampa Bay Times*, the *New York Post*, the *Star Tribune*, and the *Chicago Tribune*. Of course, the mere presence of horoscopes in major newspapers is not a reliable measure of the extent to which those who read them believe in the invisible influence of celestial bodies. According to a 2019 poll, the majority of those living in the United States (54%) read their horoscope just for the fun of it while maintaining their horoscope "doesn't really mean anything" (Jackson 2019: 2). Yet even if the majority of Americans view astrology as a form of entertainment, one in five Americans overall and nearly one in three Americans aged 18–34 consult their horoscope not only for pleasure but also because they believe it can help them "understand parts of their life" (ibid.). According to a 2018 Pew Research Center report, 29% of those living in the US believe in astrology, whether or not they consult horoscopes or only view these as sources of entertainment (Pew 2018).

A Pew report on religion in Latin America indicates a similar percentage of Latin Americans (30%) believe in astrology with highest levels of belief occurring in Nicaragua (46%) and Panama (41%) and lowest levels of belief occurring in Uruguay (20%) and Brazil (23%). But belief in astrology is not limited to the Americas. A 2014 Pew report on religion in Western Europe indicates that 23% of Western Europeans believe in astrology with highest levels of belief occurring in Spain (37%) and Portugal (35%) and lowest levels of belief occurring in Norway, the United Kingdom, and Italy (19%) (Pew 2018a). Levels of belief are even higher in India where, according to a 2021 Pew report, 44% of Indians believe in astrology, with highest rates of belief occurring in South India (51%) and lowest rates occurring in West India (32%) (Pew 2021). If levels of belief in astrology in the Americas, Western Europe, and India are any indication of global levels of belief, then it stands to reason that a significant percentage of the global population believes celestial bodies have invisible effects on human life.

Magic

A significant number of fully modern persons also believe in the efficacy of magic and witchcraft. In Latin America, 13% of the population (over 80 million people) indicated that they believed they or someone close to them had been the victim of witchcraft or black magic (Pew 2014). Rates of belief in magic are even higher in Eastern Europe. According to a 2017 Pew report, 34% of Eastern Europeans believe in "magic, sorcery, or witchcraft", with highest rates of belief occurring in Latvia (54%), Ukraine (49%), and Russia (44%) and lowest rates occurring in Hungary (14%) and Poland (18%) (Pew 2017). In India, 39% of the population (around 538 million people) agree that "magic, sorcery, or witchcraft can influence people's lives" (Pew 2021) and according to a recent poll, 21% of those living in the United States believe that magical spells and witchcraft are real (Jackson 2021). Pew Research Center reports also show that belief in the "evil eye" or the "notion that certain people can cast curses or spells that cause bad things to happen to others" is prevalent in contemporary societies (Pew 2021: 207). Once again, nearly half (46%) of all Latin Americans believe in the evil eye, with highest levels of belief occurring in Panama (64%) and lowest levels occurring in Bolivia (33%) (Pew 2014). The same percentage (46%) of Central and Eastern Europeans believe in the evil eye with highest rates of belief occurring in Greece (66%) and lowest rates occurring in Hungary and the Czech Republic (21%) (Pew 2017). The percentage of those who believe in the evil eye is somewhat lower in sub-Saharan Africa (39%) and considerably lower in Western Europe (16%) (Pew 2018a) and while belief in the evil eye was not included on questionnaires for the general US population, 39% of Hispanics living in the US report believing the evil eye (Pew 2014). Given that nearly half the population of India believes in the evil eye (49%), it appears as though hundreds of millions of people all over the world believe that curses are real and that invisible magical forces are at work in their lives (Pew 2021).

Ghosts

Although survey data on the belief in ghosts and spirits is more limited than the data on belief in astrology and magic outlined above, there is nevertheless evidence that a significant number of those living in the United States, in Latin America, and in Britain believe that ghosts are real, that certain spaces can become haunted, or that it is possible to interact with spirits of various kinds. In fact, despite the widespread idea that modernity and disenchantment should progressively reduce belief in ghosts and spirits, the percentage of those living in the United States who believe that ghosts exist appears to be growing rather than declining. Whereas Gallup polls indicate that only a quarter (25%) of the US population reported believing in ghosts in 1990, this number had risen to nearly a third (32%) in 2005 (Kambhampaty 2021). Interestingly, in 2005 an even larger percentage of the US population reported believing in haunted houses (37%) than in ghosts (32%) (Moore 2005). By 2021, over a third (36%) of those living in the US reported believing in ghosts, while 43% reported not believing in their existence (Jackson 2021). But even if a small majority of those living the US do not believe that ghosts exist, a significant and seemingly stable portion of the US population nevertheless remains unsure about whether or not ghosts are real.

In 2005, for instance, 48% of the population reported explicitly not believing in ghosts, while 19% indicated they were unsure whether or not ghosts exist (Moore 2005). In 2022, however, only 43% of the population reported explicitly not believing in ghosts, while 21% indicated they were unsure whether or not they exist.

Belief in ghosts is certainly not limited to the United States. A poll conducted in Britain, shows that 38% of British population believed in ghosts in 2007 but as there are no newer reliable polls of that population, it is unclear whether belief and uncertainty about ghosts is also growing in that context (IPSOS 2007). A significant number of people living in the Americas also believe not only that ghosts exist but also that it is possible to interact with ghosts and spirits. Nearly a quarter of the US population (24%) reports having actually seen a ghost (Jackson 2021), and 28% of Latin Americans believe that it is possible to communicate with spirits, with highest levels of belief occurring in Panama (46%) and Chile (39%) and lowest levels occurring in Ecuador (19%). Additionally, 22% of Latin Americans report having experienced or witnessed evil spirits being driven out of someone, and over a third of those living in the Dominican Republic (43%) Honduras (36%), and Nicaragua (35%) report having done so (Pew 2014).

Other Supernatural Forces

Aside from believing in the invisible influence of celestial bodies, the efficacy of magical spells, and ghosts, a significant percentage of those living in the United States and in Western Europe – both typically viewed as thoroughly modern contexts – report believing in other supernatural forces as well. For instance, 28% of the US population reports believing in supernatural beings other than ghosts, vampires, and werewolves and 7% of the population or about 23 million people report believing that vampires and werewolves exist (YouGov 2022). A significant percentage of the US population (42%) also believe that "spiritual energy can be located in physical objects such as mountains, trees, and crystals" (Pew 2018: 10), with 5% of the population (about 16 million people) reporting that they have "experienced the healing power of crystals" (Jackson 2021: 2). While belief that spiritual energy is located in physical objects is lower in Western

Europe overall (23%), significant numbers of Europeans nevertheless believe in spiritual energy including nearly half (49%) of the Spanish population and over a third of the populations of Portugal (37%) and Belgium (35%) (Pew 2018a).

As was the case when considering empirical evidence for enchantment in premodernity, it is worthwhile to consider the limitations of the available evidence for modern enchantment. Although each of the polls cited above used large random sample sets and are therefore statistically reliable, most included simple yes or no questions. While some polls included a third option for those who were unsure of their answer, this methodology nevertheless creates a simple binary between believing or not believing. As I explain in the final chapter, belief in general, but especially belief in magic and other enchantments, is likely more nuanced and complex than can be demonstrated by simply agreeing or disagreeing with a given proposition. For instance, individuals may be more likely to believe in ghosts (or less likely to disbelieve in them) at particular times of the year (e.g. Halloween), in particular contexts (e.g. while visiting an allegedly haunted house), or when interacting with specific persons (e.g. someone who claims to be a spirit medium). More importantly, it is not always clear how survey respondents interpret the terms included in survey questions. In the case of a respondent who answers "yes" to the question "have you experienced the healing powers of crystals?", it is unclear whether this respondent believes the healing powers are caused by supernatural (magical) or natural means (e.g. a positive psychological reaction). Nor is it clear that specific terms have identical or even similar meanings for respondents in different contexts. Terms such as "spirit" and "magic" may have very different connotations for respondents living in the US and those living in Latin America, India, or elsewhere. Yet even if survey data cannot provide a perfect account of levels of belief in astrology, magic, ghosts, and other enchantments, the account it does provide is clearly at odds with the one provided by the disenchantment thesis.

The negative appraisal of human emotion and experience in modernity provided by the disenchantment thesis also seems to be at odds with contemporary measures of human happiness and meaning. Whereas proponents of the disenchantment thesis posit a modern world that is flat and empty, a recent World Happiness Report shows that globally humans report experiencing positive emotions twice as often as negative ones (Helliwell et al. 2022: 16). Although the COVID–19 pandemic led to a slight increase in negative emotions, it also led to a "global upsurge in benevolence" as measured by a marked increase in the numbers of those who donate to charity, help strangers, or do volunteer work worldwide (ibid.: 7). Likewise, while proponents of disenchantment imagine a modern world that is devoid of fullness and meaning, a recent Pew survey conducted in seventeen economically developed countries shows that modern humans find meaning and fullness in various aspects of their lives including their family, friends, occupations, and in their interactions with nature and animals (Pew 2021a).[1] Given the difficulty involved in measuring fullness and meaning in premodernity, it is impossible to know whether or not humans living in the modern world encounter more or less meaning in their lives than their premodern counterparts did. Yet given the available recent data on human happiness and meaningfulness, it seems unlikely that the modern world is as bereft of meaning as proponents of disenchantment suggest. As I explain in Chapter 4, scholars who argue for the apparent re-enchantment of the world describe many sources of modern meaning and fullness from sports and digital technologies to natural spaces and fictional literature.

Disenchanted Religion

The disenchantment thesis is not concerned only with describing the apparent disappearance of magic and changes to emotion and lived experience in modernity. Weber, Taylor, and Gauchet also use disenchantment to describe increased rationalization and immanence within religion as well. Put simply, the disenchantment of religion involves an increasing repudiation of magic within religion itself, especially within Western Christianity. The premodern past posited

---

1. The seventeen countries surveyed were Australia, Belgium, Canada, France, Germany, Greece, Italy, Japan, the Netherlands, New Zealand, Singapore, South Korea, Spain, Sweden, Taiwan, the United Kingdom, and the United States.

by the disenchantment thesis is therefore a world in which the following are thought to be true: invisible forces exist and impinge upon humans, meaning and fullness are more accessible, and religion itself is enchanted. Yet any attempt to determine either the extent to which premodern religion was enchanted or whether modern religion is disenchanted is complicated by the fact that many of the terms and concepts used by proponents of disenchantment apply to the kinds of beliefs and practices that tend to be categorized as "magical", as well as to those labelled "religious".

Max Weber, for instance, describes enchantment in terms of interactions with spirits, yet both magical spells and religious prayers include references to posited supernatural entities. Likewise, Charles Taylor describes feeling open to otherworldly influences as a key feature of the enchanted premodern "porous" self, yet such influences occur within contexts that tend to be described both as magical (e.g. the evil eye) and as religious (e.g. religious revelation). In order to gauge how magical (or enchanted) religion is either in premodernity or in modernity, it is necessary first to clearly differentiate magic from religion. Unfortunately, there are no universally accepted criteria for doing so. Scholars have put forward multiple competing criteria, though none seem particularly well-suited to the task of determining whether religion has in fact become disenchanted in modernity.

Many influential theorists of religion in the nineteenth and twentieth centuries defined religion in opposition to magic. Émile Durkheim (1858–1917), who, along with Max Weber, was one of the founding figures of the academic discipline of social science, famously defined religion as a "unified system of beliefs and practices relative to sacred things ... which unite into a single moral community... all those who adhere to them" (1915: 62). What differentiates religion from magic in Durkheim's view is the fact that magic "does not result in binding together those who adhere to it, nor in uniting them into a group leading a common life" (ibid.: 60). Whereas religion is by definition linked to society for Durkheim, magic is a solitary affair. Yet Durkheim's communal vs. solitary criterion is not particularly helpful in determining whether or not any given example of religion is magical. *Any* moral community with a unified system of beliefs relative to sacred things is, by Durkheim's definition, a religion no matter the specifics of its beliefs or practices. Although Protestants may have criticized Roman Catholicism for its "magical" practices (saintly intercession, relics, etc.), Catholicism is, by this definition at least, no more magical than Protestantism or than any other moral community with a unified system of beliefs and practices relative to sacred things.

Sir James George Frazer (1854–1941), an influential anthropologist and author of *The Golden Bough: A Study in Magic and Religion*, defines religion instead as the "propitiation or conciliation of powers superior to man [*sic*]" (1940: 50). While magic also engages with superhuman powers, Frazer argues that magic "treats them exactly in the same fashion that it treats inanimate agents ... it constrains or coerces instead of conciliating or propitiating them as religion would do" (ibid.: 51). For Frazer, religion and magic entail by definition different attitudes toward and interactions with posited supernatural agents. Frazer's propitiation vs. coercion criterion is more helpful than Durkheim's in comparing specific examples of religious belief or practice. From Frazer's perspective, if a given Catholic believes that an image of a saint necessarily brings good luck through a kind of coercive power, her belief is magical. If she believes instead that good fortune is a product of God's will, her belief is religious. Within Christianity at least, there have certainly been official attempts to criticize the view that power inheres in objects themselves. However, official religious conceptions are often at odds with popular practices. Thus, while Protestantism may have officially rejected the notion that power inheres in particular objects, many Protestants nevertheless continued to believe that certain objects such as Bibles and prayer books were powerful in themselves (Scribner 1993: 483–484). Moreover, the idea that certain objects are in some way powerful is widespread within a variety of social structures that typically earn the designation "religion" whether this involves Daoist amulets, images of the Buddha, or religious icons in Hinduism. In order to employ Frazer's propitiation vs. coercion criterion, it is necessary to know how a given group conceives of its interactions with superhuman powers. Yet given the huge variety of belief within any religion, this task seems at best difficult and at worst impossible.

Marcel Mauss (1872–1950), a French sociologist and ethnologist, also defined religion and magic in contradistinction to one another in his influential book *A General Theory of Magic*. Mauss disagrees with Frazer's definitions, noting that magic can involve the supplication of superhuman powers, as well as their coercion (Mauss 1950: 21). Instead, Mauss accepts Durkheim's view that magic is absent from organized systems (or churches in Durkheim's terminology) and adds that what separates magic from religion is the fact that magical rites are secret, mysterious, and prohibited. The prohibition against magic is, for Mauss, its defining feature. As he puts it, "this prohibition marks the formal distinction between magical and religious rites" (ibid.: 22). Once again this seems to provide a straightforward criterion for distinguishing religious from magical practices: any rite or ritual that is socially acceptable is religious, while any rite that is prohibited is therefore magical. But this criterion is useless if the task is to determine whether religion itself has become disenchanted (i.e. less magical) in modernity as any religious rite or practice is likely to be seen as socially acceptable – at least by those who practice that particular religion.

Finally, Bronisław Malinowksi (1884–1942), an influential Polish anthropologist and ethnologist, developed a psychological interpretation of magic and argued that magic serves to meet the psychological needs of individuals rather than those of society as a whole. Malinowski argued that individuals resort to magic when faced with "the domain of unaccountable and adverse influences" (Malinowski 1954: 29). Whenever practical knowledge is insufficient or when a given situation is considered especially risky or dangerous, individuals turn to magic to enhance their "faith in the victory of hope over fear" (ibid.: 90). This focus on the practical realities of human existence led Malinowski to define magic as a means to a specific end and religion as an end in itself. As Malinowski puts it, "while in the magical act the underlying idea and aim is always clear, straightforward, and definite, in the religious ceremony there is no purpose directed toward a subsequent event" (ibid.: 38). Malinowski's criterion distinguishes between instrumental (magical) acts and non-instrumental (religious) ones. From this perspective, any attempt to achieve real-world results via supernatural means constitutes magic. Yet any number of typically religious acts including prayers for the health of family members would be magical according to this criterion. Even an eventual admittance into heaven or the attainment of nirvana – both seemingly religious goals – are directed toward a subsequent event and are therefore magical. Malinowksi's criterion can easily be applied to any religious group and yet, by this measure, nearly all of what is typically called religion would in fact constitute magic and the vast majority of those who consider themselves to be religious would instead be magical practitioners.

Given this brief overview of theoretical distinctions between magic and religion, it is clear that "magic has played a central role in scholarly efforts to define the nature of religion and to demarcate its proper bounds" (Styers 2004: 6). Yet not all scholars agree that religion and magic can be meaningfully separated from one another either in practice or in theory. In his description of religion in pre-modern Britain, Steve Bruce defines religion as "beliefs, actions and institutions which assume the existence of supernatural entities with powers of action ..." and notes that this definition "does not attempt to distinguish between religion and magic ..." (Bruce 1997: 668). Likewise, in his book *The Western Construction of Religion*, Daniel Dubuisson considers whether magic and religion can be distinguished from one another using any reliable criterion and asks, "in the name of which scientific criteria has it been decided that magic, divination, astrology, horoscopes... do not belong to the religious sphere? In point of fact, no scientific criterion can be invoked" (Dubuisson 2003: 73). Yet unless magic and religion can be clearly distinguished from one another, it is nonsensical to ask whether religion in modernity has indeed become disenchanted or unmagical. As I explain in the next chapter, many scholarly attempts to distinguish magic from religion are typically normative enterprises that exclude, often by definition, any practice, belief, or indeed individual that is deemed undesirable by whoever is drawing the distinction.

Conclusion

In this chapter I considered some of the empirical evidence for both premodern enchantment and modern disenchantment in order to determine whether the disenchantment thesis provides an accurate description of historical developments or merely a plausible but ultimately fictitious narrative. While each of the three theorists whose views I described in the first chapter assume that important changes have taken place in the beliefs, practices, and emotional lives of modern humans and that these changes mark an important rupture with the past, none of them provides any reliable evidence in support of this assumption.

Because time travel has not yet been invented, anyone who wishes to understand the beliefs and lived experience of premodern humans must attempt to reconstruct these using the available evidence. Although there is certainly textual and archaeological evidence that premodern humans wrote about magic and produced objects that might reasonably be called magical, it is difficult to determine whether or not belief in the efficacy of such magical formulae or objects was widespread or taken-for-granted among the general population, as well as whether such beliefs affected their emotions and lived experience. While it may be the case that premodern individuals typically lived lives in which fullness and meaning were more easily accessible, it also seems likely that they faced at least some of the same sorts of doubts and problems faced by modern humans. Again, knowing one way or the other is difficult. This difficulty, combined with the evidence that at least some premodern individuals actively doubted the efficacy of magic certainly does not constitute proof that the premodern world was not enchanted. However, the burden of proof lies with whoever is making an extraordinary claim and not with the person casting doubts on its validity.

Because it is possible to ask modern individuals whether or not they believe in invisible forces, magic, or spirits, determining whether or not disenchantment has in fact occurred is much easier. Belief in astrology, magic, ghosts, and other supernatural forces is by no means universal in modern society, yet it appears as though such beliefs are relatively commonplace and that a significant number of modern individuals believe in the very supernatural forces, influences, and entities that are typically associated the premodern enchanted world. Of course, "disenchantment" can be interpreted as designating a process rather than an historical event (Josephson-Storm 2021). In that case, the presence of such beliefs over a century after Weber coined the term may simply indicate that disenchantment is an (as yet) unfinished but nevertheless real process. Another plausible explanation for the widespread presence of beliefs, practices, and experiences that are typically considered "enchanted" in the modern world is that disenchantment never happened. From this perspective, disenchantment describes a desired but imaginary modern world rather than our actual contemporary reality. Without knowing to what extent premodern humans experienced fullness or meaning, it is impossible to judge whether the emotional or experiential changes that disenchantment describes have actually taken place. However, there is certainly evidence that modern humans do seek out and experience fullness and meaning. As I explain in Chapter 4, this seemingly universal drive toward meaning and fullness is a key idea explored by proponents of re-enchantment.

Whether or not disenchantment provides an accurate account of historical changes or whether it merely presents instead a mythical description of modernity, the idea that we have somehow overcome "primitive", "backward", or "childish" superstitions to become increasingly rational and developed (if also potentially angst-ridden) is pervasive both in scholarship and in popular accounts of the modern world. This narrative has become a key feature of the self-image of modernity or what I have elsewhere referred to as the "modern imaginary" (Cuthbertson 2016). In the next chapter, I consider enchantment and disenchantment not as apparently neutral descriptions of historical events but rather as ideological weapons that have been and continue to be wielded in support of various attempts to marginalize, disqualify, dispossess, and control specific individuals and groups.

Chapter 3

Enchantment and Exclusion

... each one of us as we grew up has had to take on the disciplines
of disenchantment, and we regularly reproach each other for our
failings in this regard, and accuse each other of "magical" thinking ...

Charles Taylor, *A Secular Age*

[Magic] belongs in its main principle to the lowest known stages of
civilization, and the lower races, who have not partaken largely of
the education of the world, still maintain it in vigour.

Edward Burnett Tylor, *Primitive Culture*

Disenchantment entails various constitutive *others* and yet the term
enchantment is rarely used to describe these. Instead, scholars
describe the kinds of beliefs and practices that disenchantment has
apparently displaced or eliminated using a variety of terms including "supernatural agents", "mysterious forces", "invisible influences", and, more commonly, "magic" or "superstition". As Charles
Taylor notes, the term superstition is often used to designate "the
enchanted dimension of religion, the rites and cults and practices
which partook of magic in their understanding" (Taylor 2007: 239).
Indeed, both magic and superstition have been and remain essential concepts for defining the proper bounds of acceptable religious
belief and practice both within religions themselves and also in scholarly definitions and descriptions of religion (Dubuisson 2016). Yet
despite their centrality in both theological and theoretical accounts
of religion, both terms have been and continue to be used as pejorative markers of difference. As Jonathan Z. Smith argues, "the most
common form of classifying religions, found in both native categories
and in scholarly definitions, is dualistic and can be reduced, regardless of what differentium is employed to 'theirs' and 'ours'" (Smith
1998: 276). According to this logic, whereas "our" religion is true,

legitimate, and acceptable, "their" religion is instead false, illegitimate, and unacceptable or – worse still – "their" beliefs and practices do not even earn the designation "religion" and are instead mere magic or superstition.

In this chapter, I briefly trace the history of the terms magic and superstition in order to show how each common descriptor of enchantment has been used to mark specific beliefs and practices as unacceptable, dangerous, and as worthy of exclusion. First, I outline how religious discourse has used both magic and superstition to exclude unacceptable beliefs and practices. Next, I explore how the meaning of both terms shifted after the Enlightenment such that both magic and superstition became markers of credulity, faulty reasoning, and intellectual inferiority rather than religious unacceptability. Finally, I show how discourse surrounding magic, superstition, and by extension enchantment works to exclude particular groups and individuals including religious individuals, indigenous persons, people of colour, women, and children from the standard model of a modern, intelligent, and rational human being. In other words, as Sara Mahmood might put it, individuals cannot inhabit the labels "magical", "superstitious", or "enchanted" indifferently, but must bear the consequences and exclusion these inhabitations entail (Mahmood 2010: 294 n19).

Magic, Superstition, and Religion

Although today scholars employ "magic", "superstition", and "religion" in seemingly value-neutral ways, each of these terms originally depended upon value-laden distinctions between acceptable and unacceptable practices and beliefs that arose in contexts that typically earn the designation "religious". In each of these contexts, religion (however it was conceived) was presented as good, appropriate, and desirable while superstition and magic (however these were conceived) were presented instead as bad, inappropriate, and as something to be avoided.

Antiquity

Whereas today the word superstition is often used to describe irrational beliefs (e.g. that the number thirteen is unlucky), it was originally used to describe unacceptable or overly enthusiastic interactions with gods.[1] The root of the English word superstition is the Latin *superstitio*, which is a translation of the Greek word *deisidaimonia*. Theophrastus (*c*.370–285 BCE) provides an early description of what superstition entails in the context of Greek antiquity. In one of a series of character sketches, Theophrastus describes the superstitious man (*deisidaimōn*) as someone who performs strange and unnecessary rituals (e.g. sprinkling himself with water or holding a laurel leaf in his mouth all day) and who is extravagant or immoderate when sacrificing to the gods (Martin 2004: 21–26). Plutarch (*c*.46–119 CE), who wrote a treatise on the subject of superstition, agrees with Theophrastus that superstition involves extravagant interactions with the gods but adds that many superstitious practices originate in barbaric (i.e. non-Greek) contexts (ibid.: 94). Yet while superstition is negatively depicted as foolish or else barbaric in the Greek context, it developed additional pejorative connotations in the context of Roman antiquity where it became not only a marker of extravagance but also of malicious intent and political subversion.

As was the case with *deisidaimonia*, writers in Roman antiquity sometimes used the Latin word *superstitio* to describe immoderate but relatively harmless beliefs and practices. Pliny the Elder (*c*.24–79) describes burning overly expensive incense as *superstitio* (ibid.: 129). Yet Roman writers also used *superstitio* to describe beliefs that were not only immoderate and extravagant but also false and malicious. For instance, *superstitio* was used both to describe false beliefs about the gods' abilities and attempts to call upon the gods for inappropriate reasons (e.g. to cause injury) (ibid.: 126–9). The notion of harm was also sometimes used to distinguish magic from superstition in the Roman context. Whereas for Pliny the Elder superstition involves

---

1. Although both *superstitio* and *desidaimonia* were also used to describe acceptable piety, each term eventually became more commonly associated with excessive enthusiasm and impropriety.

false beliefs and associated extravagant practices, magic involves efficacious but immoral attempts to harm people (ibid.: 130).

The first explicit distinctions between religion (*religio*) and superstition also occur in the context of Roman antiquity. Whereas *religio*
described appropriate and socially acceptable interactions with the
gods, *superstitio* described inappropriate beliefs and behaviours. As
Dale B. Martin puts it, in the Roman context, "*superstitio* is *religio* or
something that looks like *religio* used for base or even evil purposes"
(ibid.). Eventually, the term superstition described not only inappropriate religion but also beliefs and practices that threatened Roman
power and society. It is in this sense that Roman writers attacked
early Christians not as practitioners of a false or misguided religion
(*religio*) but instead as something else entirely – as proponents of a
dangerous and politically subversive superstition.

Early and Medieval Christianity

Although early Christians were originally persecuted as purveyors
of base superstition by non-Christian Romans, by 380 CE Christianity
had become the official religion of the Roman Empire. As a result,
by the end of the fourth century CE, Roman *religio* was defined by
Christian doctrine and any beliefs and practices that did not align
with Christianity were by definition excluded from the term religion. At the same time and in this new Christian context, the term
"religion" began to take on some of its more contemporary connotations and was used to describe specific church-sanctioned beliefs
and practices rather than a more general appropriate attitude toward
the gods. The meaning of "superstition" also became narrower and
was used to describe non-Christian (i.e. pagan) beliefs and practices
including the very pre-Christian Roman practices that had once
earned the designation *religio*. As was the case in pre-Christian Rome
and Greece, superstition continued to be used as a pejorative term
– as a marker of difference, of inferiority, and, along with the term
magic, of evil or demonic influence as well.

The Christian theologian Origen of Alexandria (*c*.185–253 CE) put
forward an early example of the association between superstition,
magic, and demons within Christianity. Before it became (within

Christianity at least) an inherently negative term, the term "demon" (*daimonas* in Greek, *daemonium* in Latin) referred broadly to lesser supernatural beings, including minor local deities and the spirits of dead heroes. In pre-Christian Greek and Roman thought, demons were largely viewed either as essentially good or else as morally neutral even if they might, like gods, inflict harm on human beings as retribution for injustice. But for Origen and for later Christians as well, demons were understood instead to be inherently and absolutely evil. According to Origen, demons caused disease and natural disasters, inspired the persecution of Christians, and were responsible for heresy within Christianity itself. Furthermore, because Christianity is monotheistic, Origen describes supernatural beings that had previously been viewed as gods in their own right by non-Christian Greeks and Romans (e.g. Zeus/Jupiter) as demons and as therefore intrinsically evil (Martin 2004: 177–180).

Origen also associates demons with magic, noting that magicians derive their power from demons. According to Origen, the three magi who visit Jesus in the Christian gospel of Matthew (2:1–12) do so in order to determine why their demonic magical powers are failing (ibid.: 178). Later influential theologians including Augustine of Hippo (354–430 CE) and Thomas Aquinas (1225–1274 CE) also link magic and other apparent superstitions with evil demonic influence. For Augustine, human beings learn how to perform magical rites only through evil demonic intervention. Furthermore, while magicians may use natural objects (plants, stones, etc.) in magical rites, the efficacy of such rites derives not from these objects but instead from the power of demons (Kieckhefer 2014: 50). Augustine also associates divination with demons, though he argues that demons are able to aid humans in performing divination only because, as incorporeal beings, they possess natural abilities that humans do not (Cameron 2010: 82–83). Thomas Aquinas agrees with Augustine that both magic and divination are demonic but adds that all attempts at both magic and divination are necessarily harmful, given the fact that demons always wish to deceive human beings (ibid.: 98). Later theological works linked a whole host of superstitious practices, including the use of protective charms and amulets with demonic activity, arguing that the apparent efficacy of any charm or amulet required demonic intervention and that even well-intentioned individuals entered into implicit pact with a demon whenever they made use of such objects (ibid.: 106–110).

The relatively straightforward association between superstition, magic, and demons began to shift somewhat within Catholicism during the Renaissance. Some Renaissance Catholics were critical of received religious tradition and also challenged the efficacy of accepted religious ceremonies within Catholicism. The Dutch philosopher and theologian Erasmus (c.1466–1563 CE) argued that true piety involved a movement away from visible objects and ritual actions, ridiculed the use of Christian charms and amulets as superstitious, and criticized Catholic priests who undertook rituals for financial motives (Cameron 2010: 150–155). Additionally, the rise of Neoplatonism led some Catholic writers not only to prefer spiritual realities over physical objects and ritual action but also to reconsider the straightforward link between magic and demons put forth by Thomas Aquinas (ibid.: 147).

The relationship between Christianity, magic, and superstition during the millennium between the advent of the Catholic Church and the Protestant Reformation is more complex and varied than can be described in this brief overview. While magic continued to be viewed as essentially demonic according to official church doctrine, church officials including bishops and priests were nevertheless accused of practising divination, performing magic, and interacting with demons (Maxwell-Stuart 2011). In 1303, for instance, the Bishop of Coventry and Lichfield in England was accused of "kissing the backside" of a devil and of speaking to him many times (ibid.: 19). While most pagan charms and amulets were viewed as dangerous and demonic, monks nevertheless created Christian healing charms on which Jesus' name or the names or other Christian figures replaced those of pagan gods as one component of larger efforts to Christianize pagan Europe (Scribner 1993: 481). But amulets were not used only in Christianization efforts. As late as 1470, Pope Paul II proclaimed that *Agnus Dei* pendants – made from a cross, coral branch, and animal tooth – could help women in childbirth, eradicate sin, and combat natural disasters (Musacchio 2005: 144). Some Christian writers even argued that demon worship was acceptable. Around 1370 Ramón de

Tárrega wrote a text entitled *On the Invocation of Demons* in which he argued that demon worship was permissible since demons were beings created by God and that it is therefore "permitted to worship and honour demons ..." (Maxwell-Stuart 2011: 57). Yet while debates continued concerning which sorts of practices were superstitious or magical and which were not, both terms were nearly always used to set apart illicit, dangerous, and heretical beliefs and practices from those that were sanctioned or permitted by the Catholic Church.

Reformation and Post-Reformation Christianity

The Protestant Reformation caused a significant shift in the meaning of both superstition and magic within Christianity. Protestant reformers began to use both terms to describe beliefs and practices deemed illicit and condemned by the Catholic Church, as well as those deemed acceptable.

Martin Luther (1483–1546) criticized the veneration of saints within Catholicism, described Christian pendants such as the *Agnus Dei* as the devil's sacraments, and argued that the consecration of specific objects (churches, altars, etc.) within Catholicism was essentially useless (ibid.: 160–173). The notion that the veneration of saints constituted a form of superstition, paganism, or idolatry also became a central theme in later Protestant thought (ibid.: 209). John Calvin (1509–1564) argued that Catholics understood Church sacraments to be magical incantations, described standard Catholic beliefs and practices such as the doctrine of substantiation as superstitious, and mocked the consecration of bread during Holy Communion as a kind of magic trick (Styers 2017: 18). Later Protestants also described Catholic priests as literal magicians and associated common Catholic practices (e.g. crossing oneself) with magic by claiming that they were commonly used by dangerous conjurers, enchanters, and sorcerers (Cameron 2010: 209–210). Yet although the Protestant Reformation shifted the object of critique and disparagement from practices deemed illicit within Catholicism to ones that were sanctioned by the Catholic Church, the entirely negative associations that adhered to both superstition and magic remained essentially the same.

Although criticisms of Catholic belief and doctrine existed within Catholicism before the Protestant Reformation, Protestant dissent nevertheless intensified debates within the Catholic Church concerning whether and to what extent specific ideas and practices were acceptable. After the Protestant Reformation, Catholicism underwent its own long process of reform. For the most part, Catholicism defended itself against the criticisms put forward by Protestant reformers. At the Council of Trent (1545–1563) the Catholic Church reaffirmed many of the beliefs and practices rejected by Protestants, including transubstantiation, the veneration and consecration of bread in Holy Communion, and the veneration of saints, images, and relics (Eire 2016: 381–382). Likewise, earlier associations between magic and demons remained intact within Catholicism. In terms of magic and superstition, however, one consequence of the Catholic Reformation was the more stringent dismissal of an even larger number of doubtful or potentially superstitious popular customs within lay Catholicism. Catholic theologians also accused Protestant Reformers of being heretics and consorting with demons, arguing that Protestants were themselves responsible for an apparent increase in sorcery and witchcraft (Cameron 2010: 237). Protestants were also routinely demonized in lay Catholic belief and legend. According to one rumour, when Martin Luther died, all the demons suddenly left all those they had been possessing in order to pay their respects to him at his funeral (ibid.: 238).

Other Contexts

Thus far, I have focused exclusively on the evolving distinctions between religion, magic, and superstition, along with the specific exclusions these distinctions entail within Western thought and especially within Christianity. To some extent, this Eurocentric and Christocentric focus aligns with arguments put forward by influential proponents of disenchantment. Charles Taylor's account of disenchantment, for instance, relies primarily on examples taken from European and Christian sources. Likewise, Max Weber primarily associates disenchantment with Protestantism and also views disenchantment primarily as a Western development:

> For the various popular religions of Asia, in contrast to ascetic Protestantism, the world remained a great enchanted garden, in which the practical way to orient oneself, or to find security in this world or the next, was to revere or coerce the spirits and seek salvation through ritualistic, idolatrous, or sacramental procedures.
>
> (Weber 1963: 270)

Yet reformers in non-Western contexts have made similar distinctions between religion, magic, and superstition, with comparable exclusions of enchantments deemed dangerous, idolatrous, or misguided.

In India, religious reformers such as Rammohun Roy (1772–1833) and Dayananda Sarasvati (1824–1883) described the worship of images of gods within Hinduism as superstition and idolatry and argued such superstitions led to moral depravity and were inimical to a modern rational society (Salmond 2006). During the Meiji era in Japan, Buddhist leaders such as Inoue Enryō (1858–1919) sought to modernize Buddhism by removing "superstitious" elements including magic, curses, exorcisms, omens, and astrology. For Inoue, religion referred to a system of true beliefs directed toward "the absolute" rather than this-worldly concerns or practices while "superstition" referred instead to delusions concerning non-existent things (e.g. magic) and to associated ignorant practices (e.g. curses) (Josephson-Storm 2006). In China, there were similar distinctions between appropriate religion and inappropriate superstition. During the Nanjing Decade (1927–1937), the Nationalist government defined acceptable religion as being largely symbolic and in service of the nation, rejecting popular Chinese practices as irrational, unscientific, and superstitious. As a result, the Nationalist government criticized a number of superstitious practices, including fortune telling, spirit mediums, astrology, and magic (Nedostup 2009). Within Islam as well, Muslim scholars and reformers such as Muhammad 'Abduh (1849–1905) and Rashid Rida (1865–1922) sought to integrate scientific rationality with Islamic thought by criticizing popular superstitious and magical healing practices and providing scientific explanations of both Quranic miracles and popular beliefs. For instance, Rashid Rida argued that the apparent efficacy of the evil eye was, in fact, caused only by a kind of hypnotism (Eneborg 2014).

In each of these non-Christian contexts, the terms superstition and magic marked specific beliefs and practices as improperly religious, irrational, dangerous, and deserving of excision or exclusion.

Magic, Superstition, and Scientific Rationality

Views on both magic and superstition shifted in important ways both during and after the Enlightenment. While magic and superstition continued to be seen as dangerous and problematic, criticisms were increasingly developed with reference to reason, science, and eventually to psychology. In part, this is because during the Enlightenment "secular, scientific reason largely displaced religious authority as the main arbiter of what constituted superstition" (Bailey 2013: 239).

Although a number of Enlightenment thinkers continued to describe superstition in particular as "improper religion", what made religion proper had more to do with the extent to which any given belief or practice was deemed rational and beneficial to society rather than the degree to which it was sanctioned by religious authorities. Both Thomas Hobbes (1588–1679) and John Locke (1632–1704) argued that excessive or irrational religious beliefs and practices constituted superstition and that such problematic beliefs and practices interfered with the proper functioning of society (Styers 2017). In his essay *Of Superstition and Enthusiasm*, David Hume (1711–1776) presented moderate civil Protestantism as a model for proper religion and argued that superstition involved a morbid dependence on ritual action and religious authorities, encouraged tyranny, and threatened civic peace (Cameron 2010: 303–304). Likewise, Voltaire (1694–1778) advocated a rational form of religion based on the notion of justice, criticized superstition as involving erroneous and irrational beliefs, and argued that superstition encourages sectarian violence and dangerous fanaticism (Styers 2017: 21).

Enlightenment thinkers criticized magic and superstition not only because these were antithetical to rational religion and a properly functioning society but also because they viewed belief in magic and other superstitions as misguided and foolish. Voltaire argued that superstition was unreasonable and dangerous since it permitted unscrupulous persons to deceive and control the simple-minded (Cameron 2010: 309). He also claimed that the belief in witchcraft in particular was put forward by charlatans who wished to deceive people for their own gains (Jortner 2017: 71). Other writers including the French playwright Laurent Bordelon (1653–1730) and the English essayist Joseph Addison (1672–1719) ridiculed belief in magic and other superstitions in their satirical depictions of foolish, deluded, and superstitious characters (Cameron 2010: 298–302). Similar views developed in the early American Republic. Although magic and witchcraft had both certainly been taken seriously in the American Colonies – a fact demonstrated in part by the Salem witch trials in the late 1690s – later American thinkers ridiculed belief in magic and witches. In political texts, plays, and works of fiction, American writers in the 1800s described those who believed in magic and witchcraft as credulous and deluded. As in Voltaire's writing, magic and superstition were described as being promoted by charlatans, and accounts of alleged witchcraft in particular were increasingly understood to be merely "efforts by conniving politicians and crafty churchmen to exercise control over ignorant masses" (Jortner 2017: 71).

During the Scientific Revolution, important changes concerning human knowledge and the development of what would eventually constitute the scientific method reshaped the meaning of superstition and especially magic. Francis Bacon (1561–1626), often described as "the father of modern science", argued that true knowledge could be produced by the careful observation of the natural world. Indeed, rather than dismissing magic outright, Bacon argued that apparently magical occurrences should be carefully studied as such phenomena may have natural and perfectly rational causes. For Bacon, superstition involved intellectual errors caused by a mistaken understanding of causality (Josephson-Storm 2017: 49–50). Although Bacon also claimed that superstition was the result of problematic emotional states including pride, sensuality, and fear, his approach marks an important turn toward conceiving superstitious beliefs as a fundamental error in reasoning rather than a product of mere credulity (Styers 2017: 19). The relationship between science and magic in early scientific thought is complex. As Jason Josephson-Storm has carefully demonstrated, many leading scientific figures were themselves deeply interested in magic and the occult. Largely credited with developing a mechanical view of the universe, Isaac Newton (1642–1726) also wrote texts on alchemy and magic. Francis Bacon, too, described magic as a variety of science (Josephson-Storm 2017).

Later theorists also explored both the idea that magic and science are closely related to one another and that magic involves flawed reasoning. For Bronisław Malinowski, because magic involves attempts to "dominate nature directly", it is "akin to science" (Malinowski 1954: 19). Yet Malinowski also notes that, whereas science is founded on experience and reason, magic is founded instead on desire and hope (ibid.: 87). For James George Frazer, the magical view of the world in which specific causes necessarily and inevitably lead to specific effects is "identical with that of modern science" (Frazer 1940: 49). Yet despite this basic similarity, Frazer also describes magic as a "spurious system of natural law", a "false science", and "the bastard of science" (ibid.: 11, 49). For Frazer, unlike scientific thought, magical thinking involves faulty reasoning or the "mistaken application of the very simplest and most elementary processes of the mind" and is practised by "the dull, the weak, the ignorant, and the superstitious" (ibid.: 54–5). For Edward Burnett Tylor (1832–1917), an influential English anthropologist, both magic and science depend upon the basic principle of the association of ideas, which he describes as lying "at the very foundation of human reason ..." (Tylor 2010: 104). Yet Tylor adds that the principle of the association of ideas is also responsible for human "unreason" as well (ibid.). For Tylor, magic involves mistaking *imagined* associations and connections with real ones. As a result, Tylor describes magic as an "elaborate and systematic pseudo-science" and belief in magic as "one of the most pernicious delusions that ever vexed mankind [*sic*]" (ibid.: 122, 101). Although theorists such as Malinowski, Frazer and Tylor primarily discuss magic rather than superstition, as Randall Styers notes, in many scholarly theories of magic, "comparable types of rational error or fallacy were seen as underlying both superstition and magical thinking, and any distinction between the two effectively collapsed ..." (Styers 2017: 24).

Psychologists also associate magic and superstition with faulty mental processes. Sigmund Freud (1856–1939), an influential psychologist and the founder of psychoanalysis, argues that magic results from mistaking imagined connections with real connections. For Freud, magical thinking results from a tendency to believe that what someone wishes or hopes will happen will actually come to pass – a tendency he associates with "primitives", children, and with modern neurotic individuals (Styers 2004: 171–172). Later psychologists also associated magical thinking with both "primitives" and children. Jean Piaget (1923–1980), an influential psychologist known for his work on child development, uses the term "animism" to describe the failure in both primitives and children to differentiate between mind and matter. For Piaget, this inability to separate mental and non-mental realities is at the source of primitive magic (Piaget 1973: 193). Although Piaget notes that magical beliefs in children and primitives are not identical, he nevertheless argues they resemble one another closely (ibid.: 157). B. F. Skinner (1904–1990), an American psychologist and a pioneer of behaviourism, described the behaviour of humans and other animals as the products of specific stimuli and conditioning. For Skinner, superstitious behaviours and belief in magical causality are conditioned responses. In his article "'Superstition' in the Pigeon", Skinner notes that pigeons who are rewarded with food while performing particular random gestures repeat these gestures as if they caused the food to appear even when no actual causal relationship exists. Skinner also notes that the superstitious rituals performed by card players attempting to change their luck along with behaviours exhibited by bowlers who continue to move their bodies as if they can control the ball once it has left their hands are similar conditioned responses based on false causality (Skinner 1948).

As this overview demonstrates, the terms "magic", and "superstition" have a long history of being used as pejorative markers of difference by religious individuals, philosophers, social critics, anthropologists, psychologists, and others. As a result, the various enchanted beliefs and practices these terms describe have often been viewed as undesirable, barbaric, dangerous, idolatrous, demonic, misguided, ridiculous, irrational, primitive, or childish.

Exclusions

The labels "enchanted" or "disenchanted" are not merely descriptive; they entail normative claims that often produce practical and political consequences. Specific individuals and groups who are deemed enchanted (magical, superstitious) have been and continue to be excluded from the privileges and rights enjoyed by modern subjects who are viewed instead as intelligent, rational, and disenchanted. As Randall Styers notes, terms like magic and superstition have often been used to describe groups "posing the spectre of disruption: women, children, people of color, members of lower social classes, other deviants" (Styers 2004: 16). In this section, I briefly describe groups that have commonly been labelled unacceptably enchanted and trace some of the consequences this labelling entails. Although each of the groups I describe have also been excluded on the basis of other perceived markers of difference (religion, indigeneity, race, sex, age, socio-economic status etc.), my focus here is on the particular use of magic and superstition as markers of difference and exclusion.

Religious Individuals

As I explained above, descriptors of enchantment including magic and superstition are often used to disqualify individuals and groups as being improperly religious or irreligious. Yet for many anthropologists in the nineteenth and early twentieth centuries, religion was seen as something that was disappearing owing to the pressures of modernization and secularization. As Tomoko Masuzawa notes, religion became increasingly associated in European scholarship with all those who were unlike modern rational Europeans: non-Europeans, Europeans of the premodern past, uneducated rural populations, and the superstitious urban poor (Masuzawa 2005: 19). In other words, religion itself came to be viewed as problematically enchanted.

Additionally, following the growth and popularization of atheism and of atheist critiques of religion, religious beliefs and practices in general have increasingly been described as mere magical thinking, irrational superstition, or as dangerous delusions (Dawkins 2006). The influential and outspoken atheist Sam Harris (b. 1967) describes religious belief as "absurd", as involving "fantastical notions", and "ancient superstitions", and argues that even moderate religion is a threat to human rationality, progress, and peace (Harris 2005). In contemporary critiques of religion, while atheist or sceptical individuals are typically depicted in positive terms as rational and mature, individuals who are apparently under the sway of dangerous enchantments are instead portrayed negatively as childish, unintelligent, unscientific, irrational, and violent (Ryan 2014: 49–52). Whereas superstition was once used within religions to disqualify individuals and groups as impious, in a growing number of atheist invectives against religion, the term is used instead to describe religious beliefs as irrational and potentially violent.

Indigenous Persons

Indigenous populations were routinely described as "savage" and "primitive" because, to non-indigenous eyes, they lacked material wealth, were insufficiently industrious, and therefore required the civilizing influence and control of colonial powers. Written in support of American imperialism in the Philippines, Rudyard Kipling's poem *The White Man's Burden* epitomizes the view that Western colonialism and imperialism were positive civilizing forces. In his poem, Kipling describes imperialism as a moral obligation and describes its targets as "sullen peoples, half devil and half child". Yet Indigenous persons and groups have also been deemed inferior and in need of paternalistic control and management because of their perceived superstitious, magical, and therefore "backward" natures.

While nineteenth-century anthropologists advanced negative depictions of "primitive" magic, such descriptions were also common in popular accounts. Writing in *The North American Review* in 1866, the American historian Francis Parkman describes the religious beliefs of North American Indians as involving "a chaos of degrading, ridiculous, and incoherent superstitions". He goes on to describe indigenous communities as "swarmed with sorcerers, medicine-men, and diviners", and notes that among the Hurons and Iroquois there are an "incredible number of mystic ceremonies, extravagant, puerile, and often disgusting, designed for the cure of the sick ..." (Parkman 1866:

3, 8). Given these observations, Parkman adds, "it is obvious that the Indian mind has never seriously occupied itself with any of the higher themes of thought" (ibid.: 9). An interview with Daniel Dorchester, who was then Superintendent of Indian Schools, published in the *New York Times* in 1892, describes Pueblo Indians as "victims of the darkest superstition", and as "poor subjects for education" (New York Times 1892). Likewise, an article published in 1887 in the Canadian newspaper *The Globe and Mail*, notes that although "primitive" Indians possess "manly qualities such as courage, fortitude and power of endurance", even their most exalted spirituals ideas are "embedded and wrapped up in grotesque and hideous superstitions" (Globe and Mail 1887). The article also describes Indigenous Canadians as "childishly superstitious" (ibid.). Combined with other negative descriptions of Indigenous populations, negative appraisals of Indigenous persons as superstitious are part of the legacy of Indian reservations and residential schools in both the United States and Canada.

People of Colour

As I outlined above, descriptions of beliefs and behaviours deemed magical, superstitious, and irrational marked people of colour as "primitive" and "traditional", thus requiring intervention by colonial powers (Styers 2004). Similarly, in the United States during the nineteenth and early twentieth centuries, scholarly and popular publications alike commonly described "negro" superstition and magic in ways that marked non-white Americans as inferior to their white counterparts. Articles providing descriptions of a wide variety of "negro superstitions" and "negro sorcery" regularly appeared in the *New York Times* during this period, and their authors often portrayed the beliefs and practices of black Americans in negative terms. Such negative descriptions were, of course, not limited to the *New York Times*. In a newspaper article published in *The Times* in Selma, Alabama in 1884, the unnamed author notes,

> Negroes in this section, even in their most enlightened circles, have never gotten rid of that lowest order of superstition common to the race since the birth of their most ancient forefathers, which is a firm belief in and practice of what has been called vodooism [*sic*].
>
> (Quoted in Anonymous 1890)

Similarly, in an article on superstition published in *Scientific American* in 1905, the unnamed author begins by noting that superstition is prevalent among many Americans but warns that it is especially common in the South owing to "the association and influence of darkies", before adding "there is no more superstitious class than the southern negro" (Scientific American 1905). Descriptions of "negro" superstition and magic were also very common in academic articles produced by American folklorists in the nineteenth and twentieth centuries. While many of these descriptions were less overtly racist than those that appeared in newspapers, contemporary American folklorists have recently criticized their field for its role in propagating racist depictions of people of colour and in supporting imperialism, white supremacy, and systemic racism (Prahlad 2021; Roberts 2021). Descriptions of people of colour as enchanted have also long found purchase in specific racist policies. In the United States, the architects of racial segregation viewed magical practices associated with black Americans as "irrefutable evidence of a dangerous unreason disqualifying blacks from political responsibility" (Cox 2015: 242–243).

Women

Associations between women, magic, witchcraft, and superstition have a long and complex history. Medieval European texts on magic and superstition described women as being particularly prone to disseminating superstitions because they were seen to be more credulous, impressionable, and talkative than men. Women were also said to be more likely than men to engage in witchcraft and sorcery because, lacking physical strength, they relied on magical defences and because their physical natures made them susceptible to fantasies and mental disturbances (Cameron 2010: 115–116). Women were also routinely thought to be morally and intellectually weak and therefore more likely to be tempted by demons. Combined with other factors, such views on women contributed to their being disproportionately accused and convicted of witchcraft during the "Witch Craze" of the late sixteenth and early seventeenth centuries (Jones and Zell 2005: 48). Links between women, irrationality, and superstition occur in later philosophical writing as well. John Locke describes errors concerning religion and morality as having their source in the doctrines put forward by superstitious nurses, old women, and foolish maids (Walker 1990). Likewise, David Hume describes women as weak, timid, and as addicted to superstition (Battersby 1981: 308).

Although many different kinds of arguments were made both for and against the enfranchisement of women in the United States and elsewhere, some of these arguments relied on the notion that women were especially prone to superstition in order to exclude women from voting rights. In a sermon made in 1894, a Baptist pastor argued that the enfranchisement of women would "upset the human fabric", adding that if women are given the right to vote, society will be "flooded with unintelligence, superstition, and lawlessness ..." (New York Times 1894). In a review of Oliver Maddox Hueffer's *The Book of Witches* published in the *New York Times*, the anonymous reviewer notes, "as the first woman was the first witch, the first witch was the first suffragette" (New York Times 1909).

Elderly women in particular are often associated with superstition and magic. The phrase "old wives' tales" speaks to the association between old age and problematic enchantment as does the stereotypical depiction of witches as "old crones". But scholarly accounts of superstition have also focused on the superstitions of elderly women as well. In accounts of the superstitions among residents of the Ozarks in northern Arkansas and southern Missouri, folklorists have described magical practices of the Ozark "granny-woman". As Otto Ernest Rayburn, a prolific collector of Ozark folklore puts it, the "old granny-woman ... mixes superstition with science ..." and adds, "no one is better qualified than an old midwife to report on ... superstitious lore" (Rayburn 1959: 145).

Children

As I explained above, the superstitions that are typically associated with "primitives" have also been described as childlike. An obvious corollary of calling enchantment childish is the notion that children are especially prone to magical thinking and superstitions. As Charles Taylor notes, although modern buffered selves feel invulnerable when facing the world of spirits and magic forces, these nevertheless can "haunt us in our dreams, *particularly those of childhood*" (Taylor 2007: 548, my emphasis). Because the persistence of superstitious beliefs is often seen to indicate a lack of necessary intellectual maturity, the persistence of superstition and magical thinking in children is sometimes seen as a cause for concern. An article published in *The Journal of Experimental Education* notes with some alarm that although "the rise of the scientific method ... has dispelled the animistic influences... many superstitions, embodying these animistic conceptions are still very prevalent among our school children" and finds that superstition is caused by "an unfavourable socio-economic status, inadequate mental development, lack of social adjustment, and insufficient personality adjustment" (Keurst 1939: 261, 267). The apparent childishness of enchanted beliefs and practices is also a significant motivating factor for attempting to disenchant oneself and others.

The Allure of Disenchantment

Because the label "enchanted" is often associated with irrationality, childishness, and credulity, it serves as a convenient tool for excluding individuals or groups from an ostensibly rational modern position. Although disenchantment may entail negative effects such as angst or a lack of fullness, the label "disenchanted" is nevertheless associated with maturity, reason, and science. Given the value placed upon reason and science in modern society, modern humans face significant social pressure to actively disenchant the world by dismissing magic, superstition, and enchantment as foolish, misguided, or absurd (Hanegraaff 2003: 377). In this view, disenchantment is not merely a passive societal development but an activity that humans undertake in order to position themselves as sufficiently rational and modern. As Charles Taylor notes, modern individuals are subject to disciplines of disenchantment that encourage us to criticize others for their deluded or mistaken enchanted beliefs or practices (Taylor 2007: 28). Engaging in disenchantment is perhaps even an obligation in contemporary secular society since, according to Taylor, "both science and virtue *require* that we disenchant the world ..." (ibid.: 131, my emphasis).

Although disenchantment may be a necessary activity for humans who wish to claim moral and intellectual superiority and appear sufficiently modern and rational, it is an alluring activity as well. Actively engaging in disenchantment is attractive because demystifying illusions and challenging outdated beliefs and customs are often viewed as meaningful, necessary, and worthwhile processes in themselves. But disenchantment is also enjoyable. As Herbert De Vriese puts it, "there is a perverse pleasure in taking away someone else's most cherished illusions, for it proves that we have the theoretical superiority to see through them and the practical maturity to live without them" (De Vriese 2010: 423).

Conclusion

In this chapter I have argued that enchantment, which is often described using the terms magic and superstition, has been used as a pejorative marker of difference that distinguishes individuals and groups who are imagined to be modern and rational from irrational and potentially dangerous *others*. I briefly traced the negative connotations associated with both "magic" and "superstition" as these evolved in religious discourse, philosophy, anthropology, psychology, and in popular accounts before listing and describing specific groups that have been excluded or disqualified in various ways by virtue of being labelled magical or superstitious. Finally, I explained some possible motivations for excluding individuals and groups with reference to their imagined enchanted natures including societal pressure and sheer enjoyment.

In the same way that disenchantment carries both positive connotations (maturity, rationality) and also negative ones (angst, emptiness), enchantment can designate both problematic and potentially dangerous beliefs and practices (magic, superstition) and also a range of positive feelings including fullness, joy, and wonder. Accepting the basic premise that disenchantment has taken place and that it involves both rationality and an associated sense of emptiness, a number of scholars have described the apparent re-enchantment of the world. In these accounts, the enchantment that has returned in the wake of disenchantment is one that maintains the positive rational aspects of disenchantment, while also providing avenues for wonder and fullness. The next chapter provides a description of this particular variety of re-enchantment – one in which the joy of enchantment is not marred by credulity, irrationality, or immaturity.

Chapter 4

Rational Re-enchantment

... there are, in the modern age, fully secular and deliberate strategies for re-enchantment, of which ... no one, however hard-bitten he or she may be, need feel ashamed.
Joshua Landy & Michael Saler, *The Re-enchantment of the World*

In recent decades, a number of scholars working in a variety of fields have described the apparent re-enchantment of the world. For some, this re-enchantment involves the return of magical beliefs and practices along with a renewed interest in invisible supernatural forces. I explore this take on re-enchantment in the next chapter. But for many others, re-enchantment refers instead to heightened emotional and affective states that result from human interactions with nonhuman animals and natural settings; cultural products such as novels and sports; and technological developments including computers, the Internet, and virtual reality. In this view, re-enchantment does not involve a return to Max Weber's "mysterious forces", Charles Taylor's premodern "porous self", or to Marcel Gauchet's "sacral dependence". Instead, this variety of re-enchantment describes the return of wonder, delight, and fullness to an otherwise fully rational and disenchanted modernity. This particular variety of re-enchantment has been described as "disenchanted enchantment" (Sizemore 2018), "secular re-enchantment" (Chaudhary 2019), and the "antinomial" approach to enchantment (Saler 2006). I use the term "rational re-enchantment" to describe the view that re-enchantment primarily involves heightened emotions and affects rather than a return of magic or the supernatural.

In this chapter, I provide an overview of the theoretical framework that supports this view of re-enchantment, focusing primarily on the work of Michael Saler and Jane Bennett. I also outline some specific arguments for secular re-enchantment put forward by a number of scholars working in different fields. Borrowing from Jane Bennett's description of the various potential sources of enchantment, I organize these accounts of secular re-enchantment into three general categories: culture, technology, and nature (Bennett 2001: 172). For each category, I provide a brief outline of the specific variety of disenchantment that is apparently being reversed by rational re-enchantment. However, many of the sites of rational re-enchantment that I describe push past the limits of this neat categorization and involve instead a mixture of natural, cultural, and technological aspects.

Theoretical Framework

Scholarly descriptions of rational re-enchantment often depend upon the portrayals of enchantment put forward by Michael Saler and Jane Bennett. Saler's view that modern re-enchantment constitutes a deliberate strategy to encourage both wonder *and* rationality underlies many scholarly descriptions of the didactic functions and beneficial effects of apparent re-enchantment. Although Bennett focuses on "magical sites" that are *already present* in the modern world rather than re-enchantment *per se*, her particular view of enchantment as involving natural, cultural, and technological sites in which the marvellous and its attendant positive emotions and affective states erupt in everyday life has been influential in scholarly work on modern enchantments and rational re-enchantment (Bennett 2001: 8).

Enchantment and Rationality

Michael Saler (b. 1960) describes a specific form of re-enchantment, one that is fully compatible with modern rationality and self-reflexivity and therefore "delights, but does not delude" (Saler 2006: 702). In their edited volume *The Re-enchantment of the World*, Michael Saler and Joshua Landy clearly distinguish the variety of re-enchantment they have in mind from "the periodic resurgence of traditional ideas and practices", the "sporadic generation of new creeds", or the "lingering enchantment" associated with superstitious or magical "survivals"

(Landy and Saler 2009: 2). For Saler, this view of re-enchantment as rational and as involving delight without delusion arises from a particular understanding of the relationship between modernity and enchantment (Saler 2006).

According to Saler, theorists have typically employed one of two distinct approaches when describing the relationship between modernity and enchantment: either a binary or a dialectical one. Saler uses the term "binary approach" to describe much of the theoretical work I described in the first chapter. In this approach, modernity is conceived as involving increased rationality and secularization and enchantment is conceived as involving an irrational or dangerous belief in spirits, gods, and invisible forces. From the perspective of the binary approach, modernity inevitably leads to disenchantment or the expulsion of magical and superstitious beliefs and practices. While magical or superstitious beliefs may persist in modernity, the binary approach marginalizes these, views them as residual phenomena that are both subordinate to and explicable by rationality and science, and associates such beliefs with groups that are deemed "inferior" in various ways (Saler 2006: 696). Meanwhile, Saler uses the term "dialectical approach" to describe theoretical work that criticizes modernity for producing its own dangerous enchantments and as being a "mythic construct no less enchanted than the myths it sought to overcome" (ibid.: 698). From the perspective of the dialectical approach, modernity itself is oppressive and inhumane, and the enchantments it produces such as capitalism and mass culture are both deceptive and dangerous (Landy and Saler 2009: 4). The dialectical approach is most clearly expressed by Max Horkheimer and Theodor Adorno in their book *The Dialectic of Enlightenment*, which I describe more fully in the section on natural sites of rational re-enchantment below.

Saler argues that both the binary and dialectical approaches employ a problematic either/or logic: either modernity is disenchanted and both spirits and fullness are disappearing from the world, or modernity is dangerously and deceptively enchanted and modern life is structured by various oppressive and insidious power structures. Yet Saler argues there is a third way to understand the relationship between modernity and enchantment. Saler uses the term "antinomial approach" to describe more recent theoretical work that rejects both the unambiguously triumphant binary approach and the deeply pessimistic dialectical approach and views modernity as characterized instead by "fruitful tensions between seemingly irreconcilable forces and ideas" (Saler 2006: 700). From the perspective of the antinomial approach, enchantments are voluntarily chosen rather than taken-for-granted or imposed, respectable rather than superstitious or dangerous, and multiple since there are myriad ways to be delighted without being deluded (Landy and Saler 2009: 7). Saler argues that modern rational re-enchantment is the product of *deliberate strategies* to manage the "impoverished life" that results from the standard view of disenchantment (ibid. 14). Yet while Saler argues that disenchantment has in fact taken place and has caused undesirable effects, he notes that merely reverting to earlier forms of enchantment associated with a naïve belief in spirits and magic is irreconcilable with secular rationality. Indeed, according to Saler, returning to a world of magic and spirits would be both shameful and undignified (ibid.: 2, 14). Instead, Saler argues for "fully secular strategies" for creating a "disenchanted enchantment" that is consistent with secular rationality and that promotes "human flourishing" (ibid.: 11, 14).

Enchantment as Affect

Jane Bennett (b. 1957) is primarily known for developing a version of new materialism, which she describes as "vital materialism" (Bennett 2010). Broadly speaking, new materialists argue that the material world, physical objects, and assemblages are not inert or passive "things" but are in some ways "vital, self-organizing, entangled and energetic" and are therefore quasi-agents that are able to affect human subjects and each other in significant ways (Schultz 2017: 130). For Bennett and other new materialists, everything in the world, "organic and inorganic, pulses with something vital, with the capacity to become otherwise" (Greyson 2019: 64). Yet because new materialists reject the existence of immaterial spirits or gods, this vitality is produced by the interactions of matter rather than by some animating spirit or higher power. Bennett's work on enchantment in her book *The Enchantment of Modern Life* has been hugely influential for a number of scholars working on various descriptions of rational re-enchantment. Although Bennett dismisses the standard disenchantment narrative and argues that enchantment has never really left the world, her descriptions of enchantment are nevertheless routinely cited in scholarly works that describe rational re-enchantment (Bennett 2001: 91).

Bennett is interested in exploring the affective nature of contemporary enchantments along with the ways their affective force can be deployed to inspire ethical thinking (ibid.: 3). Although the term "affect" is sometimes viewed as being nearly synonymous with "emotion", more commonly the term is used to describe sensations, moods, and experiences that surpass conscious recognition. Affect has been described as "a substrate of potential bodily responses, often automatic responses, in excess of consciousness" (Clough and Halley 2007: 2) and as "the propulsive elements of experience, thought, sensation, feeling, and action that are not necessarily captured or capturable by language or... 'consciousness'" (Schaeffer 2015: 23). To describe enchantment as affect is therefore to describe how certain situations, experiences, feelings – or for Bennett, material forms – act upon subjects, *affecting* them in particular ways. While the affects enchantments produce may involve specific consciously held emotions (a particular feeling of wonder generated by some specific experience, for instance), this is not necessarily the case. Instead, enchantments may produce complex affective states that resist being straightforwardly described.

Bennett provides several different descriptions of enchantment and its effects. Given the importance of her view of enchantment for theorists describing rational re-enchantment it is worth exploring these in some detail. In keeping with her interest in the affective states that enchantments produce, Bennett describes enchantment as a "complex mood" (Bennett 2001: 37). For her, this complex mood produces particular effects: enchantment entails engagement with the world and with one's surroundings; it produces "interactive fascination", "lively and intense engagement", "acute sensory activity" and "an energetic love of the world" (ibid.: 5, 111, 10). In particular, enchantment involves appreciating the "extraordinary that lives amid the familiar and the everyday" and noticing details, colours, and sounds that had been previously ignored (ibid.: 4, 5). Although Bennett describes enchantment as a pleasurable experience or a mood of "fullness, plenitude, or liveliness", she notes that enchantment involves disruption and disturbance as well (ibid.: 5). For her, to experience enchantment is to be both "charmed and disturbed", "struck and shaken;" likewise, enchantment produces feelings that are both "pleasant" and "off-putting", "energizing and unsettling", leading to a state that includes both "joy and disturbance" (ibid.: 34, 5, 4, 159, 111). Bennett also dissociates enchantment from traditional theology, New Age religion, magic, and the supernatural and focuses instead on "natural and cultural sites" of enchantment (ibid.: 10–11, 8, 3). Moreover, in Bennett's view, enchantment is a fleeting rather than a sustained experience. In sharp contrast to Charles Taylor's description of porous premodern individuals who were apparently immersed in taken-for-granted enchantments, Bennett describes the modern world instead as "sprinkled" with sites of enchantment and pursues "moments of enchantment rather than an enchanted way of life" (ibid.: 3, 10). Importantly, these momentary enchantments are, for Bennett, not experiences that individuals passively *receive* but are rather experiences that individuals actively *create* for themselves and others. Bennett describes "deliberate strategies" for creating enchantment and describes enchantment as an "artifice" and as "something to be made" or to be "cultivated" (ibid.: 4, 10, 51).

The view of enchantment put forward by Saler and Bennett marks a radical departure from earlier conceptions of enchantment. Rather than being associated with spirits, mysterious invisible forces, or religion, enchantment is instead associated with rationality and with natural, cultural, and material reality. Instead of being an inevitable by-product of a world that is perceived to be inhabited by supernatural agencies, enchantment is a product of deliberate rational strategies. Rather than referring to illicit, dangerous, irrational, and childish beliefs and practices, enchantment marks the sensation of delight or a complex mood of fullness and plenitude. While Bennett does associate enchantment with "childhood *joie de vivre*" – "childlike excitement about life" – and notes that "children seem to be born with a capacity for enchantment", she does not suggest that enchantment is a result of immaturity. Instead, it is unashamedly enjoyed by rational and secular adults.

This new view of enchantment is at once both narrower and broader than earlier conceptions. It is narrower because it excludes enchantment's traditional sources (spirits, gods) and because, although associated with disruption and disturbance, it omits the negative effects that are typically associated with enchantment, such as delusion or immaturity. At the same time, in this view the sources of enchantment are greatly expanded. Because this view of enchantment focuses on the effects of enchantment (delight, wonder) rather than its sources, *anything* that produces the positive emotions or affects associated with enchantment is enchanting, and *any* instance of fullness or energizing liveliness constitutes enchantment. This broad view of enchantment underlies recent attempts to describe a wide variety of cultural, technological, and natural sites as sources of rational re-enchantment.

Culture

The concept of "culture" is, like many of the concepts explored in this book, complex. The term has been used exclusively in reference to "high culture", or the cultural products (literature, art, etc.) of educated elites; to non-elite cultural products and activities such as those produced within "folk culture", "popular culture", or "mass culture"; and, more broadly, to the norms, customs, and way of life of a particular society or social group (Giddens and Sutton 2021: 145). In this section, I use the term "culture" to refer to specific cultural products (e.g. fictional literature) and to popular activities (e.g. competitive sports). I also use it to describe an apparently modern disenchanted way of life or a culture of disenchantment.

Culture and Disenchantment

According to the disenchantment thesis, rationality and science have removed magic and mystery from the world, leaving modernity sterile, empty, and angst-ridden. Whereas premodern society depended on a sacred "beyond", modern society depends on faceless bureau-cracy. While our ancestors lived in a meaningful cosmos and were open to fullness and wonder, modern humans are buffered, closed to fullness, and inhabit a cold and meaningless universe. Whereas legends and myths about supernatural beings once informed cultural norms and customs, we depend in modernity upon rational argu-ments and scientific explanations, relegating supernatural beings to the realm of fantasy or science fiction. While modern cultural prod-ucts such as films may abound with fantastical creatures, ghosts, and demons, these are understood to be mere entertainment – products of Hollywood magic rather than actual magic.

From this perspective, modern culture is thoroughly disenchanted insofar as we chastise one another for foolishly holding on to irra-tional superstitions and for engaging in magical thinking. In this culture of disenchantment, we take pleasure in being able to over-come superstitions rationally, as this allows us to feel intelligent and mature and to view others as foolish or deluded. In other words, the disenchantment of the world has itself become a way of life or a cul-ture of its own. As a result, wonder and amazement tend to be seen as childish and immature. While children may be delighted by magic tricks or spooked by ghost stories, modern rational adults ought to know better and behave better. Yet a number of scholars resist this narrative of disenchantment and argue not only that wonder and delight are returning to our apparently disenchanted world, but also that the various cultural sites that produce secular enchantment also produce practical benefits that align with modern rationality.

Culture and Rational Re-enchantment

Theorists have described many cultural sites that produce rational re-enchantment, or that produce delight but not delusion. Exploring fictional literature (including Sir Author Conan Doyle's Sherlock Holmes stories; J. R. R. Tolkien's *The Lord of the Rings*; and H. P. Lovecraft's fantasy, science fiction, and horror stories), Michael Saler argues that "imaginary worlds and fictional characters have replaced the sacred groves and tutelary deities of the premodern world" (Saler 2012: 3). Importantly, he argues that the enchantment produced in such works should "secure wonder without beguiling the mind" (ibid.: 130). For Saler, readers of fictional literature access and inhabit imaginary worlds through the *ironic imagination*, which "permits an emotional immersion in, and rational reflection on, imaginary worlds, yielding a modern form of enchantment that delights without deluding" (ibid.: 30). He also uses the thought process of the fictional character Sherlock Holmes as a model of what he calls *animistic reason*. For Saler, animistic reason provides an alternative to "narrow means-ends instrumental" reason since it depends upon the imagination to imbue its objects with meaning (ibid.: 109). Finally, Saler describes interactions between readers of fictional literature in clubs and societies, in letters sent to magazines, and in online forums as *public spheres of the imagination* and argues these spheres allowed fans to think not only about fiction but also about "topical social and political concerns" (ibid.: 99). While he notes that we ought to use science and critical thinking to "counter credulous beliefs in unsupportable claims that still pervade our culture", Saler sees ironic imagination, animistic reason, and public spheres of the imagination as supporting this task (ibid.: 200). The idea that engagement with fiction and fantasy are not mere escapism but actually support critical thinking has been taken up by other theorists as well. Writing about Phillip Pullman's *His Dark Materials* trilogy, M. G. Prezioso argues both that "literary enchantment… advances the reader's cognition" and that enchantment "serves as the catalyst for intellectual engagement" and can "transform readers intellectually and personally" (Prezioso 2021: 543, 553).

Other scholarly works on the enchanted nature of cultural products and activities have also considered the practical benefits that enchantment and rational re-enchantment produce. Describing the magic tricks performed by the French stage magician Jean-Eugène Robert-Houdin as a form of re-enchantment, Joshua Landy notes these performances fostered a beneficial state of "detached credulity" in their audiences, who were able to delight at the trick without being deluded by charlatanism (Landy 2009: 110). Viewing spectator sports as a site of modern rational re-enchantment, Hans Ulrich Gumbrecht notes how sports create a "communal body" of spectators, allow us to "keep open a place for the body" in an otherwise disenchanted modernity, and can even encourage positive feelings of gratitude more broadly (Gumbrecht 2009: 153, 157, 158). Exploring how old films, especially clips of old films included in contemporary ones, can be a site of rational re-enchantment, Rachel O. Moore notes these can be used "to make people think about the past to pry open the present and change the future" (Moore 2002: 173). Finally, in his description of the yearly Burning Man festival in the Nevada Black Rock desert as a site of rational re-enchantment, Christopher Partridge notes that Burning Man creates a powerful sense of community among its attendees and permits thoughtful and serious (if also playful) critiques of modern society, especially of modern conformity and consumerism (Partridge 2004: 163–165). The cultural products and activities described by proponents of rational re-enchantment not only are sources of delight or wonder but also support critical thought and provide other specific practical benefits, while being free from delusion or childish superstition.

Technology

Until the twelfth century CE, the term "technology" was primarily used to refer to reason (*logos*) that was subordinated to craft and artfulness (*techne*). An important shift occurred after the Protestant Reformation according to which "universal, univocal methodological principles" were applied to the "arts" of fabrication. In this new framework, "technology" eventually came to designate an "experimental attitude to nature" or the products of scientific inquiry (Szerszynski 2005: 55–64). In this section, I use the term "technology" more narrowly to refer to recent technological advances including computers, the Internet, and virtual reality. Although I focus mainly on specific technological sites of enchantment and rational re-enchantment, because technology is often associated with science, I also briefly discuss how both science and technology in general have been portrayed as enchanting.

Technology and Disenchantment

Instrumental scientific rationality, increasing industrialization and mechanization, and new technological advances have often been described not only as key features of modernity but also as engines of disenchantment. When describing disenchantment in *Science as a Vocation*, Max Weber notes, "we no longer need to adopt magical means to control or pray to the spirits – we make use, instead, of technology and calculation" (Weber 2020: 17). Weber also argues the "iron cage" of disenchantment results from the "inescapability of the technical and economic conditions of machine production" (Weber 1958: 181). Charles Taylor associates "technological civilization" with instrumental reason and "the disenchantment of the world" (Taylor 1991: 94). As Stef Aupers notes, magic and technology are generally depicted as being incompatible with one another in the social sciences, and, as a result, it is often assumed that "technological experts are at the frontier of a progressive 'disenchantment of the world'" (Aupers 2009: 153). Likewise, science and technology are often associated with negative effects for modern humans. Although Michael Saler contests key features of the disenchantment thesis, he nevertheless admits "the prevalent emphases on scientific progress, technology, and instrumental reason can be dehumanizing" (Saler 2006: 693).

According to standard accounts of disenchantment, instrumental scientific rationality replaces unscientific and irrational belief in spirits and magic and produces instead a cold, mechanistic, and alienating view of the world. These thinkers commonly view the positive affective states and emotions typically associated with enchantment as incompatible with the rational detachment and objectivity required by science. While wonder, which serves as a near synonym for enchantment in contemporary work on re-enchantment, may sometimes motivate scientific research, the goal of science is precisely to "eliminate the very conditions that gave rise to wonder" (Sideris 2017: 18). Additionally, insofar as wonder is viewed as intrinsically pleasurable, wonder may stifle scientific progress. Francis Bacon described wonder as a form of "broken knowledge" and saw in wonder the mind's problematic tendency of simply enjoying itself instead of trying to gain reliable scientific knowledge of the world (ibid.).

Technology and Rational Re-enchantment

Although science and technology are often viewed as significant driving forces behind the disenchantment of the world, a number of scholars and other writers have argued that science is capable of producing the positive affects that Bennett and others associate with enchantment. In his book *The Magic of Reality*, Richard Dawkins argues that a scientific understanding of reality can be "deeply moving, exhilarating: something that gives us goose bumps, something that makes us feel more fully alive" and can be "magical" (Dawkins 2011: 21). Yet Dawkins also clearly distinguishes the magic he describes from supernatural magic which "is just fiction" and also from the magic performed by "dishonest fakes" and "charlatans" who are only "preying on people's gullibility and distress" (ibid.: 19, 21). For Dawkins, science is not only a source of disenchanted enchantment but also the preeminent source of wonder. Because fantasy literature, fairy tales, myths, and religion all encourage "false wonder", for Dawkins "science is not one way of experiencing wonder, but the only authentic way" (Sideris 2017: 36).

Scholars have also described technology in general as a site of modern secular enchantment and as an important source of rational re-enchantment. In his book *The Enchantments of Technology*, Lee Bailey describes enchantment as "a fascinating spell that takes over consciousness, a state of feeling that immerses the soul in dreamy reverie". He also argues that "enchantments necessarily pervade and feed the heart of technological culture;" and he seeks to describe "the fascinations, charms, captivations, mystiques, trances, wizardry, sorcery, and magic of technology" (Bailey 2005: 1, 17, 19). Like Saler, Bailey is not interested in returning to "archaic superstitions" and instead proposes a form of enchantment that is "tamed by rational judgment", or a "refined enchantment" that includes "emotional and imaginative power" along with a "serious, rational tone" (ibid.: 4, 2, 3). Bailey views technological culture as *already* enchanted and so does not describe a technological re-enchantment; yet while for

Bailey enchantments are "ever-present", they are also "suppressed and denied". Thus the "radical shift in consciousness" that enchantment provides requires a newfound recognition of technology's enchantments or an "awakening" (ibid.: 4, 17).

Likewise, in an article on the topic of technology adoption, Belk et al. describe the sense of wonderment associated with new consumer technologies in particular (e.g. the newest iPhone) as a site of enchantment. Citing Bennett, Belk et al. argue "new technologies have ... become ideally suited to creating these fleeting sensations of wonder, awe, and surprise" (Belk et al. 2021: 29). However, they also note that, while new consumer technologies offer joy, euphoria, and enchantment (as demonstrated in the popularity of unboxing videos on YouTube for instance), consumers are not entirely deluded by the promise of new technologies. Citing Saler, they describe the delight that new technologies produce as a disenchanted form enchantment in which a "skeptical consumer ... suspends disbelief and continuously plays along with a procession of one technological magic show after another" (ibid.: 26). While technological enchantments may be seductive, they produce a "jaded, distanced, and ironic seduction..." (ibid. 2). According to Belk et al., although consumers become enchanted when they buy a new and exciting technological consumer project, they inevitably become disenchanted as newer more enchanting products are produced. As a result, in order to become re-enchanted anew, consumers must start the cycle again by purchasing newer, better, and more exciting products.

Other scholars have also described the positive affects and emotions produced by various specific technologies as sites of both enchantment and rational re-enchantment. In his article *Augmented Reality, Artificial Intelligence, and the Re-enchantment of the World*, Mohammad Yaqub Chaudhary argues the "technologization of human perception" via virtual reality and augmented reality systems, coupled with the development of artificial intelligence, has the power to lead to "a secular re-enchantment of the world" (Chaudhary 2019: 454). Describing enchantment in terms of affective attachments, McCarthy et al. note that the Internet, cell phones, and computer games are all sites of modern enchantment (McCarthy et al. 2005). Cathy Burnett and Guy Merchant link enchantment with the emergent quality and fluid movements between multiple texts that internet searches entail (Burnett and Merchant 2018). As was the case with the rational re-enchantment of culture, the rational re-enchantment of technology produces both positive affects and practical benefits. Stef Aupers and Dick Houtman describe digital technologies such as online role-playing games, virtual reality, and the Internet as being "increasingly considered the means *par excellence* to liberate the self from worldly suffering and imperfection and to overcome the alienation of modern life" (Aupers and Houtman 2005: 9). Similarly, Julia Cook notes that fears about the long-term future in young adults are often balanced by a "sense of re-enchantment with technology" that provides "a vehicle for fostering a sense of faith in humanity ..." (Cook 2016: 520).

Nature

Like "culture", the term "nature" is complex. In this section, I use the term "nature" very broadly to describe the following: living things including plants and nonhuman animals, "natural" spaces that might be described as "wild" such as forests, and spaces in which humans regularly intervene, such as gardens. Nature understood in these broad and colloquial terms has often been viewed as source of enchantment in both senses of the word. It is a site where humans gain access to "the sacred", where magical and supernatural agents or spirits dwell, and where heightened emotions such as wonder or awe find their source.

The Disenchantment of Nature

Insofar as enchantment denotes invisible forces, spirits, and god(s), the disenchantment of nature involves rejecting the existence of sacred groves, enchanted forests, or spiritual essences that inhere in natural things such as animals or plants. However, the "disenchantment of nature" more commonly refers to a shift in human views of nature according to which nature is no longer seen as meaningful or mysterious but is instead imagined to be wholly accessible to human understanding and therefore subject to human exploitation. According to Bronisław Szerszynski, the standard narrative of disenchantment depicts nature as something that has been "progressively mechanized and instrumentalized" and is therefore "something to be counted, measured, and mapped", and a "resource to be owned" (Szerszynski 2005: 4, 5). Likewise, Alison Stone links the disenchantment of nature to "disrespectful and narrowly instrumental attitudes to nature, which are ultimately responsible for environmental destruction" (Stone 2006: 231–232).

The disenchantment of nature is a key concept explored by Max Horkheimer (1895–1973) and Theodor Adorno (1903–1969) in their book *The Dialectic of Enlightenment*. Adorno and Horkheimer describe Enlightenment as involving the advance of human thought and argue that its programme is the disenchantment of the world. For these two thinkers, disenchantment primarily involves dispelling myths and replacing fantasy with rational scientific knowledge. Yet, they see both the Enlightenment and disenchantment as deeply problematic developments. In *The Dialectic of Enlightenment*, they trace the negative effects of Enlightenment and disenchantment, arguing that they produce exploitative capitalism, deceptive mass culture, totalitarianism, and fascism, each of which ultimately leads to human enslavement and subjugation. Put simply, "the wholly enlightened earth is radiant with triumphant calamity" (Horkheimer and Adorno 2002: 1).

For Horkheimer and Adorno, the disenchantment of nature involves the "extirpation of animism" or the rejection of the notion that nature possesses a soul or spirit (ibid.: 2). Once "immanent powers or hidden properties" are removed from nature, the natural world is viewed instead, through the lenses of science and technology, as a mere "thing" to be manipulated for human ends: "[n]ature, stripped of all qualities, becomes the chaotic stuff of mere classification" and "the mind, conquering superstition, is to rule over disenchanted nature" (ibid.: 2, 3). The result is that the relationship between humans and nature becomes one of conflict, exploitation, and domination. Thus, they claim, "nature became a mere undifferentiated resistance to the abstract power of the [human] subject" and "what human beings seek to learn from nature is how to use it to dominate it wholly ..." (ibid.: 70, 2).

Nature and Rational Re-enchantment

The disenchantment and subsequent domination of nature, which has led to the degradation of ecosystems as well as catastrophic climate change, are key problems for environmentalists. What the re-enchantment of nature is often thought to offer, therefore, is a shift away from attitudes that support domination and exploitation toward attitudes that foster instead positive affective states like wonder, respect, and care. James William Gibson provides an account of re-enchantment that more closely aligns with a view of nature as animated by spirits in his book *A Reenchanted World*, arguing that the re-enchantment of nature "is nothing less than the reinvestment of nature with spirit" (Gibson 2009: 11). Yet Gibson also links re-enchantment with positive affects and emotions including plenitude, a sense of a personal connection, and being overcome with emotion (ibid.: 89). For Gibson, re-enchantment involves rejecting "modernity's reduction of animals, plants, and natural forces like winds and ocean waves to utilitarian resources", allowing us instead to "create world we really want, a world full of wonder" (Gibson 2010: 56, 60). In her book *Vital Reenchantments*, Lauren Greyson argues for a re-enchantment of nature and for "affective ecologies with wonder at their core" (Greyson 2019: 256). For Greyson, however, rational re-enchantment should involve neither "naïve animisms" nor the "glorification of technoscience" (ibid.: 49). The enchantments that she describes have nothing to do with "an unseen transcendent realm" but instead pay attention to "the miraculous, contingent unfolding of the life processes that surround us" (ibid.: 62).

Scholars have also described particular sites of natural enchantment and rational re-enchantment and have linked these to positive affects and to practical goals, such as environmentalism and environmental advocacy. Avril Maddrell describes nature pilgrimages as sources of enchantment. Citing Bennett, she describes enchantment as the feeling of being entranced, as a creative or emotional "high", and as energizing and argues, "these energising qualities of enchantment … are sorely needed in the face of the current social and environmental challenges …" (Maddrell 2022: 318). Exploring transitory and communal gardens created in inner cities as a site of rational re-enchantment, Robert Harrison notes these gardens reveal and inspire "the need to care" for living things and spaces and reinforce a "life-affirming principle" (Harrison 2009: 80). Describing sea turtle conservationists, Lori Beaman notes that they experience moments of enchantment which translate into an ethic of commitment to the survival and thriving of sea turtles (Beaman 2021: 9). Although Beaman, like Bennett, argues that the natural world is already enchanted and so does not require re-enchantment, she argues "mobilizing enchantment... can aid in responding to the climate crisis and human abuse of the planet" (ibid.: 10). Aside from sea turtle conservation, Beaman lists many other natural sites of enchantment:

> For me they come, sometimes, when listening to music, when one of the crows who lives in my neighbourhood follows me to my clothesline and chortles at me, when sparkles that that flow from my fingertips run through water with phosphorescence in it on a night time walk on the beach, or when a curious "teenage" mink whale comes up beside my rowboat in the Atlantic Ocean ...
>
> (Beaman 2021: 5)

Describing enchantment as a "spine-tingling moment of discovery or recognition" rather than as being about "ghosts, gods, and goodness", Beaman, like many who write about the enchantment and re-enchantment of nature, see the natural world as infused with innumerable enchantments (ibid.: 5, 4).

Conclusion

In this chapter I explored several different accounts of one particular variety of re-enchantment. Proponents of rational re-enchantment locate secular modern enchantments in a wide variety of cultural, technological, and natural sites from *The Lord of the Rings* to chortling crows and from Burning Man to virtual reality. What connects the accounts of re-enchantment explored above is their shared conception of enchantment. Rather than connect enchantment to spirits or mysterious forces, they link enchantment to positive emotional or affective states like wonder and joy. Focusing on the negative affective consequences of disenchantment (emptiness, angst) described by theorists of disenchantment, proponents of rational re-enchantment argue that re-enchantment involves recognizing or deliberately fostering positive affects, such as fullness and plenitude.

Yet by focusing on the *effects* of enchantment rather than its causes, the various scholars I surveyed produce a view of enchantment that is much broader than the depictions of enchantment I described in earlier chapters. In this view, *absolutely anything* that produces heightened emotions can be described as enchanting. Given this expanded definition, scholars have also described the re-enchantment of the legal profession, art therapy, the corporation, medicine, radio, behavioural psychology, geography, Englishness, terrorism, political theology, Europeans, the suburbs ... and the list goes on. Importantly, however, none of these accounts of rational re-enchantment makes any reference to spirits, god(s), magic, superstition, or other "delusions". If they do refer to magic, they do so in the sense that Dawkins employs the term, as a near synonym for wonder. In this sense the definition put forward by proponents of rational re-enchantment is also narrower, as it typically excludes supernatural sources of enchantment described by proponents of the disenchantment thesis such as spirits, invisible forces, or god(s).

Another feature that connects each of these accounts of rational re-enchantment is their insistence that the positive affective states associated with enchantment (wonder, joy) are not delusional but instead constitute a reasonable, rational, and mature interaction with secular sources of enchantment. In many of the accounts of rational re-enchantment described above, enchantment is rational, of course, but it also produces specific beneficial effects from intellectual engagement to informed critiques of consumerism and from faith in humanity to environmental advocacy. In this view, enchantment and the wonder it produces are not merely pleasant experiences but are perfectly serious, rational, and practical. In other words, proponents of rational re-enchantment seek to retain the apparently beneficial aspects of modernity and disenchantment (rationality, science, technological innovations) without accepting the more deleterious consequences that are often associated with modernity and disenchantment (emptiness, alienation, angst). I provide a more thorough critique of arguments for rational re-enchantment in the final chapter.

Other scholars have also argued for a very different form of re-enchantment. Rather than view re-enchantment as a rational project to secure wonder and create beneficial practical effects while avoiding magic and superstition, they describe re-enchantment as involving the apparent return of magic, gods, and ghosts to the modern world. I consider this very different approach to re-enchantment in the next chapter.

Chapter 5

Spiritual Re-enchantment

Magic is real, magic works, and everyone has the ability to use it.
Jennifer Hunter, *21st Century Wicca*

According to the disenchantment thesis, modern humans no longer believe in and therefore no longer rely on god(s), magic, spirits, or invisible forces. Instead, modern humans prefer scientific explanations and rely on technology. Unlike proponents of secularization who argue that religious belief and affiliation is declining or that religion is losing its social significance, proponents of disenchantment argue instead that religion itself has become disenchanted: magical and superstitious elements have been removed, immanent gods have been replaced with a distant and transcendent deity, and religion has become increasingly rationalized. As I explained in the preceding chapter, a number of scholars have proposed either that the modern world is experiencing a rational re-enchantment or else that the wonder and delight associated with enchantment have never left the world and that these affective states can therefore be fostered in various deliberate and rational ways. Other scholars describe re-enchantment differently – not as delight without delusion but as a return of belief in and reliance on gods, magic, spirits, and invisible forces. According to this version of re-enchantment, modern humans not only increasingly believe in and interact with magic and spirits, but new thoroughly enchanted forms of religion are re-enchanting the religious sphere as well.

I describe the apparent return of gods, magic, and spirits to disenchanted modernity as "spiritual re-enchantment". Given that disenchantment is often conceived of as involving the removal of spirits and magical means from modernity (re-enchantment thus involving their return), the qualification "spiritual" is not, strictly speaking, necessary. Additionally, the term "spiritual" is notoriously "fuzzy" and is defined in diverse ways both by scholars and by those who engage in various spiritual practices or describe themselves as spiritual (Zinnbauer et al. 1997). Despite these issues, I use the (admittedly imperfect) term "spiritual re-enchantment" to distinguish the version of re-enchantment outlined in this chapter from the version described in the preceding one.

I should also note that while I use "rational re-enchantment" and "spiritual re-enchantment" to distinguish between distinct scholarly approaches and to describe very different forms of apparent re-enchantment, these two categories inevitably overlap at times. Specific sites of re-enchantment such as nature, for instance, may produce both rational enchantment (delight, practical benefits) and also spiritual enchantment (the belief that nature is magical or animated by spirits). In other words, rational re-enchantment is not necessarily unspiritual. Nor is spiritual re-enchantment necessarily irrational: it would be unlikely for a contemporary Wiccan who believes in the efficacy of a magical spell, for instance, to view her own belief and practice as irrational or deluded.

In this chapter I outline the most detailed theoretical account of spiritual re-enchantment, focussing especially on the work of Christopher Partridge. I also describe a variety of "neo-pagan" new religious movements in which many practitioners both believe in and actively engage with gods, magic, and spirits. Next, I consider a range of popular alternative spiritual beliefs and practices involving contact with spirit entities and alternative healing practices that are often categorized as "New Age". Finally, I explore a renewed interest in the presence of ghosts and spirits in modern society, along with the individuals who claim to be able to communicate or interact with them.

Theoretical Framework

The version of re-enchantment that I explore in this chapter receives its clearest articulation in Christopher Partridge's (b. 1961) two-volume work *The Re-enchantment of the West*. As was the case with many of the proponents of re-enchantment that I cited in the preceding chapter, Partridge also accepts the basic premise of the disenchantment thesis. For Partridge, disenchantment is "the process whereby magic and spiritual mystery are driven from the world, nature is managed rather than enchanted, and the spiritual loses 'social significance' ..." (Partridge 2004: 11). But he uses the term "disenchantment" to refer to many other specific modern developments that scholars more commonly associate with secularization or, in the case of Charles Taylor, with secularity. In his description of the "disenchanted world in which we all live", Partridge argues,

> The decline of community, the proliferation of large, impersonal conurbations, the increasing fragmentation of modern life, the impact of multicultural and religiously plural societies, the growth of bureaucracy, the creeping rationalization, and the influence of scientific worldviews have together led to a situation in which religion is privatized, far less socially important, and far less plausible that it was in pre-modern communities.
>
> (Partridge 2004: 16)

Partridge's focus on the social significance and plausibility of religion are especially important for his overall view of spiritual re-enchantment. Because he focuses on re-enchantment in "the West", his model for religion is primarily Western Christianity, though he does discuss other institutionalized forms of religion as well. For Partridge, spiritual re-enchantment depends upon religion (i.e. Christianity) becoming less socially significant and on religious beliefs becoming less plausible as a result of secularization and disenchantment. Citing Peter Berger, Partridge describes a perennial "religious impulse" that involves a "quest for meaning that transcends the restricted space of empirical existence" (ibid.: 39). Given this basic impulse for meaning and because traditional religion has become less socially significant and less plausible, modern individuals seek out meaning in spiritual contexts *outside* the realm of traditional institutionalized religion. For Partridge, disenchantment understood in these terms is precisely what permits spiritual re-enchantment to occur: disenchantment and secularization are the necessary precursors to spiritual re-enchantment (ibid.: 43).

According to Partridge, spiritual re-enchantment describes the "variety of ways increasing numbers of Westerners are discovering and articulating spiritual meaning in their lives" (ibid.: 1). Importantly, Partridge argues this spiritual meaning is most often derived from "non-traditional" (i.e. non-Christian) sources, such as "Eastern" religions and mysticisms, paganism, and other alternative spiritual beliefs and practices (Partridge 2002: 242). He describes this variety of re-enchantment as involving "new ways of believing" that "meet the new wants and needs of new Western people" and as being "emergent" and "detraditionalized" (Partridge 2004: 1, 44, 39). Given his focus on social significance, Partridge notes that the alternative spiritual options associated with spiritual re-enchantment are neither superficial nor insignificant but are instead personally and socially consequential (ibid.: 2, 58). Although spiritual re-enchantment may involve new non-traditional varieties of belief and practice, he claims these beliefs and practices are nevertheless important both for society and for individual practitioners who engage with them.

For Partridge, the contours of spiritual re-enchantment are largely determined by the modern developments I described in the first chapter. Given the growth of individualism in modernity and the modern focus on immanent this-worldly goals rather than transcendent ones, Partridge describes spiritual re-enchantment as involving a "self-centric, immanentist ... worldview" (Partridge 2002: 248). While modern communication technologies contribute to a pluralization that weakens existing plausibility structures, they also permit the introduction and dissemination of new (non-traditional) beliefs and practices that become important resources both for contemporary spiritual seekers and for spiritual re-enchantment more broadly. Many contemporary neo-pagans and New Age practitioners, for instance, learn about neo-pagan beliefs and practices and find communities of practice online. Finally, given that a multitude of new spiritual practices and paths become available in modernity, modern individuals are also able to pick and choose from a plurality of options in order to create their own unique spirituality (ibid.: 71).

Occulture

Partridge uses the term *occulture* to describe the vast "reservoir of ideas, beliefs, practices, and symbols" which modern, spiritually re-enchanted individuals draw upon when creating their own unique spiritual paths (Partridge 2004: 84). The root of Partridge's term "occulture" is the word "occult". While "occult" originally designated something that was hidden or concealed, it eventually came to designate ancient knowledge as explored by a variety of schools and secret societies (ibid.: 68–69). Partridge argues that today "occult" is an umbrella concept for a wide variety of unusual or "deviant" ideas and practices. According to him, concepts and practices that might be described as occult include: magic, angels, spirit guides, astral projection, crystals, astrology, tarot cards, numerology, prophecies, palmistry, shamanism, goddess spirituality, eco-spirituality, Druidry, Heathenism, and Wicca (ibid.: 70). Yet Partridge uses "occulture" to describe more than beliefs and practices that are typically deemed occult. He notes that occulture also involves a focus on the autonomy of the self and on a desire for increased self-awareness that are often associated with "New Age" beliefs and practices along with a romanticization of premodern individuals and societies (e.g. premodern paganism) and a focus on achieving direct experiences of the supernatural or divine (ibid.: 71–78).

Partridge also argues that popular culture provides a collection of ideas and practices that contribute to the larger reservoir of occulture. Unlike Michael Saler, who views elements of popular culture such as fantasy, science fiction, and horror fiction as sites of rational re-enchantment, Partridge views fictional literature and films that feature occult content as potential sources for spiritual re-enchantment. Individuals who seek new concepts and practices to meet their spiritual needs may become interested in fictional representations of magic, sorcery, demons, or spirits and then incorporate these concepts into their own individual spiritual paths. For Partridge, depictions of occult practices in popular books, films, television shows, and video games also help to increase the plausibility and acceptability of occult spiritual concepts more broadly. In depicting and exploring various non-traditional spiritual concepts and practices, popular occulture not only makes these accessible to large audiences but also renders these concepts more familiar. This familiarization with alternative spiritual options helps shape new plausibility structures and worldviews in which fascination with or belief in magic, spirits, and invisible forces are taken more seriously and no longer viewed as deviant, silly, or delusional (Partridge 2002: 246). Indeed, Partridge argues that occulture challenges "official" rational and scientific accounts of reality and leads to the return of "a form of magical culture" (Partridge 2004: 40).

The new modern magical culture that Partridge describes is neither identical to premodern enchantment, nor does it necessarily fully align with scientific rationality as is the case with rational re-enchantment. He notes that, unlike premodern magic, modern magic or alternative spiritual practices may be interpreted with recourse to scientific concepts and metaphors (e.g. energy) or contemporary psychological concepts (e.g. the unconscious) (ibid.: 41). Yet, despite these updated explanations and interpretations, modern magic is not merely metaphorical or psychological. For many spiritually re-enchanted individuals and for neo-pagans in particular, magic is simply an accepted feature of reality like any other. Likewise, Partridge notes that just because modern individuals may not believe in supernatural agents in the same way that premodern individuals did, this does not mean their belief is insincere or trivial or that supernatural agents are any less real for them (ibid.: 123). While many modern individuals may engage with occultural elements purely for their entertainment value, according to Partridge, an increasing number of modern individuals draw on occultural concepts and practices in order to shape alternative spiritualities, worldviews, and definitions of reality that are significant both personally and more broadly. In the next sections of this chapter, I explore some specific varieties of magical culture and spiritual re-enchantment, including neo-paganism, alternative spiritual beliefs and practices that are often labelled "New Age", and individuals who claim to communicate and interact with spirits and ghosts.

Neo-Paganism

Neo-paganism is a term used by scholars to describe a variety of new religious movements and contemporary spiritualities such as Witchcraft, Wicca, Druidry, and Heathenism that emerged after the 1950s and that share a common interest either in recovering historical pre-Christian pagan beliefs and practices or else drawing upon these imaginatively to create new spiritual paths. Individuals who view their practice as the revival or continuation of an ancient pre-Christian religion typically reject the prefix "neo" and either use the generic term "Pagan" to describe themselves or else a more specific term that reflects the geographical region or particular variety of pagan belief on which their practice is based (e.g. Ásatrú for practices based on Norse paganism). Yet many practitioners who acknowledge instead that neo-paganism is a modern movement inspired by ancient sources and practices rather than a continuation of pre-modern beliefs also typically use terms other than neo-pagan to describe themselves (Pike 2004: 20).

Neo-pagan beliefs and practices are extremely varied and fluid. Aside from sharing a common interest in reviving, continuing, or re-imagining older pagan practices, most neo-pagans are polytheistic and believe in the existence of multiple gods. Many neo-pagans also believe in the existence of a variety of spirits, value the natural world, believe in reincarnation, engage in divination, and consider magic to be both real and effective. Many neo-pagans also report feeling alienated both from traditional religious options such as Christianity and from modern reductionistic scientific rationality and technology (Jorgensen and Russell 1999). This sense of alienation is a potential factor motivating neo-pagans to revive or re-imagine alternative spiritual options. In what follows, I outline some of the spiritually enchanted features of neo-paganism that make the growing popularity of neo-pagan belief and practice a potential site for spiritual re-enchantment.

Gods

Although some neo-pagans are monotheistic and believe in a single god or goddess, most are polytheists and believe in and interact with multiple gods. Some neo-pagans focus on a specific pantheon of gods, such as Odinists who worship the Norse god Odin along with other gods and goddesses from Norse mythology, while others include deities from a wider range of cultures and contexts. Many neo-pagans believe that gods and goddesses are present in the world rather than fully transcendent. Describing Druidry, Michael T. Cooper notes, "there is a strong sense of being in the presence of and experiencing gods and goddesses ... giving the practitioner the experience of communing with gods" (Cooper 2009: 69). Indeed, many neo-pagans describe gods in terms of experience and interaction rather than belief. Gods are often invoked or called upon in neo-pagan magic and ritual practice.

Spirits

In addition to various deities, many neo-pagans also believe in and interact with a variety of spirits. For some neo-pagans, the entire cosmos is animated by a large array of non-human spirit entities. Sometimes, these spirits are conceived as *genius loci*, or spirits of the place, who dwell in trees, rocks, and in other natural sites. Others describe spiritual entities associated with the four elements (earth, water, air, fire) in particular. Additionally, neo-pagans sometimes speak of spirit entities who live in the home. For instance, some Wiccans argue that specific household shrines should be created to house the spirits of the home (Doyle White 2015: 95–96). In her large survey of over six thousand neo-pagans living in the United States, Helen Berger found that over 80% US neo-pagans feel they had been near a powerful spiritual force at least once; over a quarter report often receiving prophecies, visions, or messages from the spirit world; and more than half reported communicating with someone who had died (Berger 2019: 107).

Magic

Magic (which is also sometimes spelled "magick" to differentiate it from stage magic) is a key component of neo-pagan belief and practice. According to Helen Berger, for most neo-pagans, magic and a sense of the world as enchanted "is an essential part of being a contemporary Pagan" (Berger 2019: 87). Many neo-pagans believe the universe is filled with a divine energy that flows through the human body and the external environment, binding all living things together in a complex magical web (Urban 2015: 173). For many neo-pagans, magic involves manipulating this energy with the mind for specific desired results through practices like meditation, rituals performed either in groups or by solitary practitioners, or spell-casting (Berger 2019). Spells can follow set procedures and involve specific required objects (e.g. a black candle, a particular stone) or else can be improvised by the practitioner. Some neo-pagans use specific magical tools in spell-casting such as an athame (a double-edged dagger), a wand, and a chalice or cup (Hunter 1998). Helen Berger notes that magical practice is very common among neo-pagans in the United States. Nearly 95% of US neo-pagans practice magic at least occasionally, and more than a third practice magic often or regularly. Additionally, most neo-pagans in the US (67%) believe that magic involves tapping spiritual energies or entities that transcend the ordinary material world, while less than 10% believe that magic is nothing more than human psychology (Berger 2019: 91).

Divination

Many neo-pagans also engage in divination practices of various kinds, such as consulting tarot cards or runes, having psychic readings performed, reading or preparing astrological horoscopes, and engaging in palmistry and numerology. According to Berger, tarot cards are the most popular form of divination among neo-pagans in the US, as over 70% report consulting tarot cards (ibid.: 100). Additionally, more than half of neo-pagans in the US take divination seriously enough to alter their behaviour as a result of information attained by divination. As I explained in the second chapter, 29% of the general US population report believing in astrology (Pew 2018). Rates of belief in astrology among neo-pagans is predictably higher, especially among women. According to Berger, 43% of neo-pagan women and 31.1% of neo-pagan men believe in the efficacy of astrology (Berger 2019: 103).

The academic study of neo-paganism is complicated by a number of factors. Because there is no central bureaucracy or group that provides an official doctrine or membership list, individuals self-identify as belonging to the various new religious movements organized under the neo-pagan label. The result is what Helen Berger refers to as a "disorganized religion" (Berger 2019). Yet owing to earlier associations between neo-paganism and Satanism, combined with the hostility some neo-pagans face from conservative Christians in the United States and elsewhere, individuals are sometimes reluctant to self-identify as neo-pagans or to "come out the broom closet" as some Witches and Wiccans put it. Although the total number of neo-pagans remains quite small, there are indications that neo-paganism is growing in the United States, Western Europe, and Canada. Whereas census data indicate there were about 5000 pagans in Canada in 1991, by 2001 this number had grown to over 20,000 (StatCan). According to the 2014 Pew religious landscape survey, there are about 1.5 million neo-pagans living in the United States (Pew 2014).

Yet according to Partridge's re-enchantment thesis, the gradual dissemination of neo-pagan belief and practice, along with increased familiarization, contributes to the larger reservoir of occultural re-enchantment, even if the actual global population of neo-pagans remains small. One example of recent neo-pagan visibility is the "Bind Trump" spell organized by Michael M. Hughes in 2017 that received considerable media attention in the wake of the 2016 presidential election. Although some neo-pagans criticized the spell and organized their own protective rituals in response, many Witches, Wiccans, Pagans and other magical practitioners gathered in both physical and virtual locations to enact the spell in an effort to magically limit President Trump's power in office (Hoo 2019).

New Age

The term "New Age" is typically used to designate a vast array of alternative spiritual beliefs and practices that gained popularity in the second half of the twentieth century in the United States and Western Europe. As was the case with neo-paganism, there is no central authority or institutional framework in the New Age Movement, nor are there any commonly agreed upon doctrines or standard texts. Given the wide variety of beliefs and practices that are commonly labelled New Age, along with the amorphous and decentralized nature of the movement, scholars often resist providing final or decisive characterizations of the movement (Lewis 1992). Broadly speaking, the beliefs and practices that tend to be labelled New Age concern channelling, a process whereby someone interacts with various non-human entities; alternative healing therapies, many of which focus on energy (e.g. chakras, auras); and the integration of contemporary scientific ideas (e.g. quantum physics) with spiritual concepts (Hanegraaff 1996).

While many New Age beliefs and practices developed out of nineteenth-century spiritual or metaphysical movements including the New Thought Movement, Theosophy, and Spiritualism, contemporary New Age beliefs and practices tend to be highly individualistic and are focused on self-growth and personal spiritual development or actualization (Albanese 1999). Individuals involved with New Age tend be interested in transforming the self through various techniques such as meditation and alternative healing practices. But New Age beliefs and practices also tend to be focused on transforming larger society through alternative understandings of physical existence and, in the case of channelling, through insights gained by interactions with perceived spiritual or extraterrestrial entities.

Because the New Age Movement shares certain characteristics with neo-pagans such as an interest in tarot, meditation, and spiritual energies, scholars sometimes include neo-paganism in their descriptions of the New Age Movement. Indeed, books focussed on Wicca and magic are often found in the New Age section of bookstores and popular gatherings such as the yearly *Starwood* festival combine both neo-pagan and New Age workshops and presentations (Pike 2004: 35). One key difference between neo-paganism and New Age is that while neo-pagans tend to look to the past in their efforts to revive or re-imagine pre-Christian paganism, New Age beliefs tend instead to be forward looking and focus on "a coming era of spiritual harmony and well-being that will transcend this current age of violence and strife" (Urban 2015: 221). Additionally, neo-pagans often seek to differentiate their beliefs and practices from the New Age Movement, which they criticize for being overly commercialized, self-centred, and simplistic (Pike 2004: 22). In what follows, I outline specific New Age beliefs and practices, including channelling and spiritual healing practices, as potential sites of spiritual re-enchantment.

Channelling

Channelling involves the process whereby an individual (a channel) receives information or guidance from sources external to ordinary consciousness or else serves as the vehicle or conduit for a variety of spiritual entities which are often thought to reside in different planes of existence (Riordan 1992: 105, Urban 2015: 221). The precise nature of these sources or spiritual entities varies greatly. For instance, Cindy Riggs, a professional channel, psychic, and healer from Ohio describes interacting with "thousands of beings" including "an Azetc woman", a "shapeshifter" who appears as both a hawk and a man, the Hindu gods Vishnu, Ganesh, and Shiva, and an entity she calls "the Oneness, which is all the light beings in the universe at once" (quoted in Urban 2015: 224–225).

There are two main varieties of channelling: conscious channelling and trance channelling. Whereas conscious channels typically interact with the entities they channel in order to receive information, trance channels usually become "possessed" by the entities with whom they interact; these entities then act and speak through them (Albanese 1999). While channels are sometimes viewed as possessing an innate sensitivity or openness to spiritual entities, channelling is also described as a skill that anyone can master. The Delphi University of Spiritual Studies in Georgia, for example, offers a channelling certification course designed to awaken intuitive abilities and allows its students to "tune in" and receive "an accurate and consistent flow of energy, guidance, and inspiration" (see https://delphiu.com).

Although channelling is controversial even for some within the New Age Movement, it has nevertheless received considerable media attention in recent decades. J. K. Knight, a channel who claimed to receive messages from a thirty-five-thousand-year-old being called Ramtha who lived in a section of the ancient continent of Atlantis called Lemuria, appeared on multiple prime time television programmes and was featured in mainstream magazines (Urban 2015). The belief in and practice of channelling spiritual entities among some New Age practitioners and the appearance of various channels on popular television programmes make channelling a key candidate for the variety of occulture and spiritual re-enchantment Partridge describes. As Suzanne Riordan suggests in *Perspectives on the New Age*, "[t]he re-enchantment of the world is both cause and effect of the popularity of a form of interdimensional communication currently known as 'channelling'" (Riordan 1992: 105).

Spiritual Healing

New Age beliefs and practices often focus on healing both individuals and society as a whole (Lewis 1992). Some New Age healing practices such as a focus on holistic health, herbal therapies, aromatherapy, yoga, and meditation are becoming increasingly mainstream. Additionally, not all New Age healing practices (e.g. aromatherapy) involve interactions with spirits or invisible forces and so are unlikely sites for spiritual re-enchantment. Moreover, some seemingly enchanted practices (e.g. crystal healing) tend to be explained in terms of physical properties or processes. In her book *Crystal Enchantments*, D. J. Conway argues that stones and crystals naturally produce particular vibrations and healing energies. According to Conway, an individual who wears a particular stone will inevitably benefit from these healing energies. She claims that agate, for instance, should be worn to cure insomnia while amethyst calms mental disorders, purifies the blood, strengthens the immune system, helps with migraines, and balances and heals all chakras (Conway 2011).

Other New Age healing beliefs and practices more directly involve subtle invisible energies and sometimes spiritual beings as well. Healing practices involving chakras (focal points in the body first described in Hindu and Buddhist texts), auras (energy fields believed to surround humans, animals, and physical matter), and Reiki (which involves the transmission of invisible healing energy) all focus on interacting with and manipulating postulated invisible spiritual energies (Albanese 2000). This focus on subtle spiritual energies is a key feature of New Age belief more generally (ibid.). Often, various ways of conceiving and manipulating spiritual energy are combined. An article posted on the website for the International Association of Reiki Professionals describes reiki as an ancient "healing art of spiritually guided universal life force energy" and claims this energy flows through particular pathways including chakras (IARP undated a). Another article on the same website describes an "attunement process" for "opening" chakras in order to access "divine energy". The same article notes that once a practitioner becomes attuned to Reiki they gain access to "spiritual gifts" and can enlist the assistance of "other higher powers" including "spirit guides, ancestors, elemental beings, Earth spirits, and angels" (IARP undated b). Energetic healing is also sometimes combined with channelling in New Age practice. Barbra Brennan, a well-known energetic healer and best-selling author of several books including *Hands of Light*, claimed to have channelled several different beings who guided her in her spiritual practice and work (Albanese 2000).

As with "neo-pagan", many of those who engage with the alternative spiritualities categorized as New Age contest this label in part because it has become associated with practices and beliefs that may seem absurd or irrational when viewed through the lens of mainstream scientific rationality. As a result, it is difficult to determine the total number of New Age practitioners. Nevertheless, New Age beliefs and practices are widely disseminated in best-selling books, television programmes, and online and are increasingly popular. In the United States, around 80% of those who list their religion as "nothing in particular", and nearly three quarters of those who identify as spiritual but not religious hold at least one new age belief (Gecewicz 2018). New Age beliefs are also popular among those involved in traditional religions as well, as nearly 60% of Christians in the United States hold at least one New Age belief (ibid.). Given Partridge's focus on occulture as a source of spiritual re-enchantment, the popularity of New Age beliefs and practices along with the incorporation of alternative and holistic therapies into mainstream medical practice are key features of a progressive re-enchantment of the Western world (Partridge 2004: 52–53).

Ghosts

While both neo-pagan and New Age belief and practice typically involve interactions with various spirits, interest in the existence of ghosts and belief in the ability to interact and communicate with the spirits of humans who have died are also increasingly popular. Contemporary belief in and apparent engagement with ghosts share similarities with movements that were popular in the nineteenth century, most notably Spiritualism. Nineteenth-century Spiritualists argued that some humans called mediums were able to summon and communicate with the spirits of the dead. Like contemporary neo-paganism and New Age, nineteenth-century Spiritualism was a decentralized movement that lacked any central institutional structure. Instead, a wide variety of mediums organized séances which could be held either in private or presented as public performances. In these séances, mediums claimed to communicate with the spirits of the dead. Séance co-participants or spectators could detect the presence of these spirits via strange events (e.g. flickering candles, knocking sounds), and mediums could do so by communicating information thought to be known only to spirit in question. While Spiritualism and séances were common in Western Europe and the United States in the nineteenth century and became a popular form of entertainment, belief in Spiritualism declined considerably in twentieth century (Urban 2015).

While the popularity of Spiritualism and belief in the ability to communicate with spirits declined in the twentieth century, there are indications that the belief in ghosts and spirit communication is growing in the twenty-first century. In the United States, a Gallup poll conducted in 1978 indicated only 11% of respondents believed in ghosts, but by 2001 that number had risen to 31%, and by 2003 it had grown to 51% (Kwilecki 2009). Like their nineteenth century counterparts, contemporary mediums also claim that they are able to communicate with the spirits of the dead, though many also profess to possess psychic abilities as well and describe themselves as psychic mediums. Contemporary mediums also put on public displays of their apparent intuitive abilities.

John Edward is a self-proclaimed medium and was the host of the popular television programme *Crossing Over with John Edward* that aired between 2001 and 2004. In his show, Edward would interact with a live studio audience and perform "readings" in which he would interact with audience members and ask questions about deceased loved ones with whom he claimed to communicate. Theresa Caputo is another well-known medium who was the focus of the popular reality television programme *Long Island Medium*, which aired on the Learning Channel from 2011 to 2019. The show depicted Caputo's daily activities along with various readings that she performed in which she contacted the spirits of the dead in public and private settings. According to Caputo, she has been "seeing, feeling, and sensing Spirit" since she was four years old and practices as a medium in order to "deliver healing messages that would help people learn, grow, and embrace life" (see www.theresacaputo.com/about-me). Scholars writing about contemporary mediums have suggested that programmes such as *The Long Island Medium* may serve to "address broader existential and unconscious fears" concerning death and may also provide a means of validating viewers' own supernatural or non-empirical experiences (Darghawth 2013; White 2019).

Contemporary interactions with ghosts and spirits do not take place only through psychic or spirit mediums; there are also a growing number of psychic and paranormal investigators in the United States and elsewhere who claim to be able to detect ghosts and remove unwanted spirits from homes. Jane Phillips, for example, who describes herself as a "psychic, medium, and paranormal investigator" offers "ghost-busting" services through her company Geyser Energy Clearing Services (see https://ghostbusting.org/about). Although the company advertises energetic cleaning services to home owners, it also offers its ghost-busting and energy remediation services to real estate agents. According to the company website, a given home does not need to be haunted in order to feel energetically "off", as energetic residue from the stressful experiences of previous owners may also be to blame (ibid.). Professional ghost removal services seem to be increasingly popular and accounts of residential ghost removal professionals such as Phillips have been published in *The Wall Street Journal*, *The New York Times*, and *The Chicago Tribune* (McLaughlin 2016;

Wadler 2008; Weigel 2010). Investigations of apparent hauntings have also been featured in popular television and streaming programmes, such as *Ghost Hunters*, which features Jason Hawes, founder of The Atlantic Paranormal Society (TAPS). *Ghost Hunters* has aired in various iterations between 2004 and 2016 and again from 2019 to the present.

Not all ghosts perceived to exist are unwelcome visitors that require investigation or removal. After-Death Communication (ADC) describes another common and less problematic way in which apparent ghosts are said to interact with humans. ADC describes a situation in which an individual feels as though a deceased loved one has communicated with them in some way. Unlike Spiritualism or mediumship, ADC describes spontaneous contact rather than contact achieved through a séance or via a medium (Drewry 2003). Perceived contact with a deceased loved one can occur in various ways, including sensing their presence, hearing their voice speaking words out loud, hearing their voice in one's head, seeing the deceased person, smelling a distinctive scent (e.g. the deceased's perfume), receiving phone calls, perceiving the otherwise inexplicable movement of household objects, witnessing natural phenomena (e.g. if an animal associated with the deceased appears unexpectedly), and experiencing vivid dreams (ibid.). ADC events typically occurs within one year after the death of loved one and have been described in multiple news stories, in popular books, and on websites (Kwilecki 2009). Unlike hauntings, ADC events are largely viewed as therapeutic, and popular books on ADC have been endorsed by bereavement organizations in the United States, such as Mothers Against Drunk Driving and Parents of Murdered Children (ibid.).

Perceived interaction with ghosts is seemingly commonplace in the United States. According to a 2021 Pew research report, while only 14% of Americans (about 46 million people) report having actually communicated with the dead, a much larger number (77%) of Americans believe it is possible to feel the presence of someone who has died, while 55% believe that a deceased person can offer help to the living (Pew 2021b). Importantly, belief in communication with the dead has risen substantially in the United States. According to the Roper Center, while only 5% of those living in the United States reported believing in after death communication in 1957, this number had grown to 14% in 1986 and to 21% in 2001 (Roper 2005). By 2021, nearly half (47%) of all Americans reported believing after death communication is possible. The popularity of spirit mediums and ghost detection and removal services, coupled with the growing levels of belief in communication with the dead, are all potential sources of spiritual re-enchantment.

Conclusion

In this chapter, I described a view of re-enchantment that focusses on the apparent return of magic, invisible forces, spirits, and ghosts to the modern disenchanted world. Unlike rational re-enchantment, which describes positive affective states and practical benefits that align with disenchanted rational and scientific explanations of the world, spiritual re-enchantment describes instead a more literal re-enchantment or re-magicking of contemporary beliefs, practices, and society. From the perspective of spiritual re-enchantment, while the modern world did experience a process of disenchantment in which belief in magic, invisible forces, and ghosts declined, this process is being progressively reversed.

Importantly, from Partridge's perspective, disenchantment is a necessary precursor for spiritual re-enchantment. For Partridge, it is precisely because traditional religious and spiritual avenues for enchantment became less plausible (owing to modernization, secularization, and disenchantment) that individuals feel the need to craft new spiritual beliefs and practices. Additionally, the dissemination of these new beliefs and practices in print media, on television, and online caused them to become increasingly familiar. Fictional representations of various occult ideas in popular culture also supported this growing familiarity. The result, for Partridge, is the creation of a vast reservoir of alternative spiritual concepts or an occulture from which modern individuals can draw in their efforts to create new enchanted beliefs and practices.

Although rational and spiritual re-enchantment provide very different accounts of apparent re-enchantment, there is some inevitable overlap in the proposed sources of re-enchantment. While I presented in the preceding chapter scholarly arguments that culture, technology, and nature are sites for rational re-enchantment, scholars have argued that there are cultural, technological, and natural sources for spiritual re-enchantment as well. Partridge, for instance, describes vampire fiction, ambient music, cyberspace, virtual worlds, eco-paganism, and eco-spirituality as sources from which the West has become spiritually re-enchanted (Partridge 2004, 2005). What distinguishes spiritual re-enchantment from rational re-enchantment is not the proposed sources of re-enchantment but rather how "enchantment" is conceived in each approach. Whereas the term enchantment describes positive affective states unaccompanied by delusional beliefs for proponents of rational re-enchantment, for advocates of spiritual re-enchantment it describes belief in various concepts, entities, or forces that tend to be labelled magical, occult, supernatural, or spiritual.

Belief is a key concept in both accounts of re-enchantment – either in terms of the lack of irrational beliefs or delusions in the case of rational re-enchantment, or else in terms of the presence of magical or spiritual beliefs and attendant practices in the case of spiritual enchantment. Belief is also a key component in descriptions of disenchantment. As I explained in the first chapter, disenchantment is often described as involving either the disappearance of certain kinds of beliefs in god(s), magic, and spirits, on one hand, or a situation in which such beliefs are no longer axiomatic, on the other. In the next chapter, I provide an alternative way in which to understand enchantment – one that rejects viewing enchantment as a matter of straightforward belief and disenchantment as a matter of disbelief and which prioritizes instead the complex ways in which contemporary individuals imaginatively, ironically, and playfully engage with ideas concerning god(s), magic, and spirits.

Chapter 6

Modern Enchantment

[Believe] is a vague predicate that admits of in-between cases – cases
such that a careful ascription requires refraining from simple attri-
bution or denial of the belief in question.

Eric Schwitzgebel, *Acting Contrary to our Professed Beliefs*

Thus far, I have provided an overview of key theoretical approaches to
disenchantment; described scholarly critiques of the disenchantment
narrative; outlined the ways in which the labels enchanted, magical,
and superstitious have been used pejoratively as markers of exclusion; and attempted to distinguish between two distinct approaches
to re-enchantment, which I have labelled "rational re-enchantment"
and "spiritual re-enchantment" respectively. In my view, while the
disenchantment thesis, doubts surrounding disenchantment, the
societal and individual pressures that modern individuals face to
avoid being seen as superstitious or deluded, and accounts of rational
and spiritual re-enchantment all provide important insights concerning enchantment, disenchantment, and re-enchantment, none
of these accounts provides a full picture of modern enchantment.

In this final chapter, I describe my own take on enchantment.
Specifically, I draw upon the theoretical frameworks discussed in
previous chapters, along with recent philosophical work on the connections and disjunctions between belief and behaviour, to propose
a novel approach to what I see as an understudied variety of modern
enchantment – a variety that I refer to as "fluid enchantment". From
the perspective of fluid enchantment, straightforward binary distinctions between enchantment and disenchantment oversimplify the
complex ways in which humans believe in and engage with magic,
spirits, and invisible forces. While some people emphatically and consistently believe in and engage with magic and spirits (e.g. "serious"

neo-pagans) and others emphatically and consistently disbelieve and therefore refuse to engage with these (e.g. New Atheists), I suspect that most people occupy a position in between these two poles. I use fluid enchantment to describe situations and contexts in which individuals partially, ironically, or playfully engage with magical or supernatural beliefs and practices without fully adhering to these beliefs and without necessarily viewing these practices as being straightforwardly effective. I begin by outlining the binary and largely implicit model of belief on which the accounts of enchantment, disenchantment, and re-enchantment outlined in earlier chapters rely.

Enchantment and Belief

The concept of disenchantment depends upon claims concerning the beliefs of both premodern and modern humans. Simply put, the standard account of disenchantment maintains that premodern humans believed in the existence of god(s), spirits, and invisible forces (i.e. magic), and because modern humans believe instead in the power of reason and in scientific explanations, belief in spirits and invisible forces has declined or disappeared. In *Science as a Vocation*, Max Weber describes disenchantment as involving "the knowledge, or belief... that in principle there are no mysterious incalculable forces intervening in our lives, but instead all things, in theory, can be *mastered* through *calculation*" (Weber 2020: 18, italics in original). Although Charles Taylor describes belief and unbelief as *lived conditions* rather than mere theories or sets of beliefs, the lived condition of unbelief fostered by disenchantment nevertheless makes belief in god(s), spirits, and invisible forces difficult to maintain (Taylor 2007: 8, 3). According to Taylor, god(s), spirits, and invisible forces become "inconceivable" in our secular disenchanted age, (ibid.: 30). Likewise, while Taylor describes the porosity of premodern porous selves "as a fact of *experience*" rather than a matter of theory or belief and notes that the modern buffered self "feels invulnerable before the world of spirits and magic forces", these experiences and feelings depend upon believing or disbelieving in the existence of spiritual entities and magic forces (ibid.: 39, 548, italics in original). Thus, the buffered self *feels* invulnerable precisely because it "begins to find *the idea* of spirits, moral forces, causal powers with a purposive bent close to incomprehensible" (ibid.: 539, my emphasis). For Taylor, the lived experience of disenchantment is, at least in part, the result of particular new beliefs about the world (Taylor 2010: 307). It is only because modern disenchanted individuals *believe* magical beliefs to be irrational or view these as incomprehensible that they are capable of "overcoming and rising out of earlier modes of belief" (Taylor 2007: 268). Modern disenchanted unbelief may be a lived condition for Taylor, but it nevertheless involves the absence of particular beliefs. As Taylor puts it, disenchantment results from "our having 'lost' a number of beliefs and the practices that they made possible" (Taylor 2010: 302).

Criticisms of the disenchantment thesis also typically rely on the presence of certain kinds of belief. In his book *The Myth of Disenchantment*, Jason Ānanda Josephson-Storm cites sociological data concerning the prevalence of paranormal beliefs in the United States and Europe as evidence that "we have never been disenchanted" (Josephson-Storm 2017: 22–28, 3). Josephson-Storm also refers to the presence of "popular belief in witches, magic, spiritualism, and angels" in early-twentieth-century Germany, as well as the fact that "many of his [Weber's] contemporaries believed in magic" in order to dismiss the standard reading of Weber's *Entzauberung* or disenchantment as referring to the straightforward absence of magical thinking in modernity (Josephson-Storm 2021: 36). Likewise, in describing disenchantment as a "regulative ideal" rather than a neutral historical process, Josephson-Storm describes the ways the myth of disenchantment pressures modern individuals "to purge or hide occult beliefs" (Josephson-Storm 2017: 312).

The exclusionary work that labels such as "enchanted" along with related terms such as "magical" or "superstitious" perform also depends upon on the presence of presumed illicit, dangerous, irrational, "primitive", or childish beliefs. As I explained in Chapter 3, after the Enlightenment, superstition became increasingly associated with deviant or irrational beliefs. Enlightenment philosophers, nineteenth and early twentieth century scholars of religion, and psychologists all described superstitious and magical beliefs as the product of faulty reasoning. The various groups and individuals excluded by this view of superstition, magic, and enchantment were criticized for their apparently aberrant beliefs. According to this (problematic) view, religious individuals are deluded, indigenous individuals are incapable of abstract thought, people of colour are subject to dangerous unreason, and women are intellectually weak. While these groups were disqualified from full participation in society for many other (equally problematic) reasons, in so far as they were described as being dangerously superstitious, they were disqualified as a result of their imagined apparently irrational *beliefs*.

Belief is also central in accounts of both rational and spiritual re-enchantment. For Michael Saler, re-enchantment is a form of disenchanted enchantment precisely because the positive affective states (wonder) that enchantment produces are balanced by rational thought and insight. Rational re-enchantment therefore produces delight without any deluded beliefs. The self-reflexivity that Saler associates with the ironic imagination likewise involves a situation in which "beliefs are held in a double-minded way, with an awareness of the interplay of truth and artifice ..." (Saler 2021: 108). Spiritual re-enchantment depends upon the recovery or articulation of specific beliefs whether these involve witchcraft and spells, channelling various entities and invisible energies, or interacting with ghosts. According to Christopher Partridge, re-enchantment involves "new ways of believing" that fit with the interests and priorities of modern individuals (Partridge 2004: 1). Partridge also describes occulture as a reservoir of ideas and argues that depictions of occult practices in popular culture serve to render occult beliefs more plausible. Although Jane Bennett and others who focus exclusively on the affective nature of enchantment are uninterested in specific beliefs, as I explain in the conclusion, discarding belief entirely from descriptions of enchantment ignores the way in which enchantment has been and remains associated with specific postulates such as the existence of magic, spirits, and invisible forces.

As Michael Saler notes, standard ways of conceiving enchantment and disenchantment depend on binary formulations: either the world is enchanted (or re-enchanted) or it is disenchanted; either someone believes in god(s), spirits, and invisible forces or she does not (Saler

2006). As I explained in Chapter 3, this binary formulation often leads to a neat division between an imagined rational, scientific, modern, acceptable *us* and an imagined irrational, primitive, pre-modern unacceptable *them*. Yet this binary might also be used by individuals who have become spiritually re-enchanted, in which case the division would be between an imagined intuitive, awakened, spiritual, and magical *us* and a cold, unimaginative, rational, and scientifically reductionist *them*.

These neat divisions between beliefs and individuals fit well with a common sense understanding of what it means to believe something. Belief itself is typically understood in binary terms: either I believe that ghosts exist or I do not; there is no middle ground. In everyday speech, the word belief is not typically used for indeterminate states. If I have never thought about the existence of ghosts, for example, it would be impossible to claim either belief or disbelief. Likewise, if I am uncertain as to whether or not ghosts exist, I would describe myself as doubtful rather than describe the presence or absence of specific beliefs. Yet I suspect that for many people, belief is not quite so straightforward a phenomenon. I suspect that it is possible to both believe and not believe something in the same respect without contradiction. I also suspect that considering various ways in which humans partially believe or half-believe sheds light on the ways modern individuals engage with enchantment and believe in magic in one form or another on a daily basis without necessarily becoming fully fledged neo-pagans, New Age practitioners, or spirit mediums.

Before exploring some philosophical accounts of half-belief and related states, I would like to briefly relate an episode from my PhD research – one that inspired my interest in varieties of partial belief and fluid enchantment. My research involved a small number of interviews with individuals who possess lucky or protective objects. One such interview was with a thirty-six-year-old woman named Amélie. Amélie is a college professor, holds a master's degree, self-identifies as an atheist, and does not engage in any religious or spiritual practices. During our interview, we spoke about a wooden fertility statue that Amélie received as a gift. Amélie explained that she had zero confidence that the statue could actually promote fertility and told me that the statue was purely symbolic. Yet Amélie also explained that she kept the statue in the living room of her home because that is where she and her husband spend the most time together and where, as a result, the statue could have the greatest effect. She also mentioned that she would be upset if the statue was lost, damaged, or stolen because she wanted to have a second child. Finally, Amélie explained that once she had her second child, she intended to give the statue to someone who intended to start a family of their own (Cuthbertson 2016). What is going on here? According to the binary view of belief, either Amélie believes the statue promotes fertility or she does not. If she *does* believe the statue promotes fertility, why would she describe the statue as purely symbolic? If she *does not* believe the statue promotes fertility, why would she place it in the living room to maximize its possible effects or intend to give it to someone who wanted to start a family?

Half-Belief

Questions surrounding belief – what belief is, how beliefs are acquired, how they are justified (or not), and whether and how beliefs can be attributed to other people – are central to philosophy and especially to epistemology, which is the philosophical subfield concerned with the study of knowledge. Recently, a number of philosophers have presented various models with which to account for partial or half-belief that may provide answers to the questions concerning Amélie that I posed above. In what follows, I outline some key philosophical approaches to partial belief before drawing on these to argue that fluid enchantment involves simultaneously believing and disbelieving in god(s), spirits, and invisible forces.

Half-Belief

H. H. Price (1889–1984), a Welsh philosopher who specialized in the philosophy of perception, put forward an account of half-belief in a symposium on that topic in 1964. Price notes that, although philosophers rarely discuss the concept of half-belief, "it is familiar to all of us" and "is a fairly common phenomenon" (Price and Braithwaite

1964: 149, 152). Price distinguishes half-belief from believing with a low degree of confidence and from believing in only half of some idea or proposition. For Price, there is nothing partial or "half-ish" about having low confidence in some potential outcome. Price uses the example of having only a moderate degree of confidence that a letter will arrive on a specific day. In Price's view, until new information is acquired (e.g. I realize the post office is closed), my moderate degree of confidence remains basically consistent. Likewise, while Price admits that it is possible to believe in only half of a given statement or theory (e.g. I believe that my friend really did visit London but suspect she is lying when she says that she drank tea with the Queen), such cases do not constitute half-belief as Price uses the term. Instead, he employs half-belief for situations in which an individual believes something only some of the time, is swept away by a particularly moving experience, or is quite literally "of two minds" about a given proposition or idea.

Price discusses religious belief and behaviour as an example of part-time belief. He imagines an individual who describes himself as religious and who believes that God exists and yet whose beliefs and related behaviours are inconsistent. In church on Sunday, this person behaves outwardly as a religious person would, experiences appropriate emotions, and strongly agrees with what is said in the sermon. The rest of the week, this person rarely thinks about God, rarely prays, and behaves in ways that run contrary to religious norms. According to Price, such a person is not a hypocrite nor is he only pretending to be religious; instead, he is in a state of half-belief. He also considers superstitions such as touching wood or refraining from walking under ladders as examples of half-belief: "the ordinary person who avoids walking under ladders does not seriously believe that walking under ladders does any harm" (ibid.: 158). Yet individuals who avoid walking under ladders or who touch wood consistently nevertheless "act as if they believed" and "show the emotional symptoms of belief", even if they "will not admit that they do believe these propositions; not even to themselves and still less in public" (ibid.: 157).

To illustrate the idea that someone can be swept away into a state of half-belief, Price imagines someone watching a particularly moving play. That person's emotions, behaviour, and intellectual activities all coincide with the reality of the play, such that it appears as though the person believes that the events on stage are really happening. Still, while the imagined theatre-goer may be deeply moved by the events on stage, reacts as if the events are real, and thinks carefully about the plot and characters, it is unlikely this person would jump on stage to intervene if, say, the hero of the play was in danger. Price notes that half-belief of this variety is more than the mere suspension of disbelief or the "neutral state of neither believing nor disbelieving" and involves instead "a state of near-belief with regard to propositions which do not correspond to actual facts" (ibid.: 155). For Price, near-belief of this variety is a product of the imagination.

Price introduces the idea that someone can be literally "of two minds" about a given proposition (e.g. that ghosts exist), while considering whether or not half-beliefs are reasonable. Typically, two criteria are used when judging whether or not a given belief is reasonable. A belief is deemed reasonable if it supported by evidence and if the strength of the belief corresponds to the strength of available evidence. A belief is also deemed reasonable if it is consistent with other beliefs (ibid.: 159). Thus, it would be unreasonable for me to believe strongly that ghosts exist if there is no evidence or only weak evidence to support this belief, and it would also be unreasonable for me to believe in the existence of ghosts if I also maintain the belief that ghosts do not, in fact, exist at all. Yet there is plenty of "evidence" that ghosts exist: a significant number of those living in the United States believe in ghosts and claim to have interacted with them, spirit mediums are featured in popular television programmes, and there are professional ghost-busters who claim to remove negative spiritual energy from residential properties. While half-beliefs may sometimes be unreasonable owing to insufficient evidence, this is not always the case. Yet it is clearly inconsistent to believe that ghosts exist while simultaneously believing that they do not exist. According to Price, this inconsistency does not necessarily make half-beliefs unreasonable. For Price, the inconsistency of half-belief is a result of "a dissociated or disintegrated personality" (ibid.). As he puts it, "with one part of his mind, the part which is operative in circumstances *A*, *B*, and *C*, he [a half-believer] believes such and such a proposition: with another part of his mind, which is operative in circumstances D, E, and F, he does not believe or even disbelieves it" (ibid.).

Price's take on half-belief demonstrates the connection between belief and context. Given particular circumstances, propositions that an individual might otherwise doubt or even reject outright become increasingly plausible. Thus, whereas I might half-believe in the existence of ghosts while listening to a ghost story, hearing strange sounds in the middle of the night, or attending a particularly dramatic séance, I might reject that same belief while speaking to a sceptical atheist friend, walking around the city in daylight, or reading an article that explains how spirit mediums use psychological tricks in their readings. In circumstances that support my half-belief in ghosts, I would demonstrate all the characteristic symptoms of belief, and in circumstances that challenge my belief in ghosts, I would sincerely and emphatically deny any such belief.

Alief

Tamar Gendler (b. 1965), an American philosopher who specializes in philosophical psychology and epistemology, also considers context or environment when considering half-belief. Like Price, Gendler is interested in accounting for situations in which an individual apparently holds a certain set of beliefs and yet acts in ways that contradict these. Rather than use the term half-belief to describe such situations, Gendler coins a new term: "alief". Gendler provides several examples of alief, or situations in which a person's behaviour fails to coincide with their firmly held beliefs. For instance, Gendler describes the case of visitors who step onto the Grand Canyon Skywalk, which is a glass walkway suspended over the canyon. Although visitors obviously *believe* the Skywalk is safe, as no one would step onto the glass walkway if they believed it was unsafe, visitors nevertheless routinely display *behaviours* that coincide with the opposing belief that both their action and the Skywalk are dangerous (Gendler 2008: 635). Gendler also describes psychological studies that show that "well-educated Western adults" often *behave* as though they believed in the laws of sympathetic magic or that properties can be transferred from one object to another, while nevertheless firmly rejecting this belief. For example, subjects are often reluctant to eat soup from a brand-new bed pan or fudge that has been formed into the shape of dog faeces, or to put newly purchased vomit-shaped rubber in their mouths despite the fact that they know *and firmly believe* the bed pan is perfectly clean, the fudge is really fudge, and the "vomit" is just plastic (ibid.).

Gendler argues that alief is distinct from both deception and self-deception. A person's behaviour may fail to coincide with their firmly held beliefs if that person wishes to deceive someone else (e.g. while bluffing in a poker game). Yet study participants who refuse to eat soup from a bed pan are clearly not attempting to deceive the psychologists studying them. Gendler also notes that in cases of self-deception, individuals typically show reluctance to endorse the beliefs they view as problematic (e.g. if I deceive myself into thinking I am more intelligent than I am, I would avoid endorsing the belief that I really am quite stupid). But someone who steps onto the Skywalk *does* fully endorse the belief that the Skywalk is safe, even if her outward fearful behaviour seems to contradict this belief.

Gendler also argues that alief is distinct from both belief and imagination. For Gendler, belief is reality-sensitive. My beliefs depend upon the world around me and while my beliefs may turn out to be mistaken, I am not free to believe whatever I choose. For instance, while I might *wish* that I was ten feet tall, it would be absurd to say I believe that I am. Imagination, by contrast, is reality-insensitive. I am free to imagine whatever I like (that I am ten feet tall, say) even if my imagination does not coincide with reality (alas, I am only five foot ten). Yet in the examples described above, alief is both reality-insensitive *and* reality-sensitive. A person's reluctance to put vomit-shaped rubber in her mouth *does not* depend on the reality of the situation or her beliefs concerning that reality (i.e. the "vomit" is only rubber and she knows this to be the case) and yet the reluctant behaviour *does* depend on specific perceived features (i.e. the rubber resembles vomit).

For Gender, alief is a mental state activated by features of a person's environment. When faced with a particular situation (e.g. vomit-shaped rubber), a person either consciously or unconsciously alieves that it is disgusting and reacts accordingly (i.e. is reluctant to put it in her mouth). Gendler argues that in paradigmatic cases, alief creates affective states and also propels the alieving subject toward particular behaviours (e.g. disgust and reluctance). Gendler also notes, however, that there may be cases of alief in which there is no obvious affective component or behavioural response. Importantly, she argues that alief can be occurrent (active in the moment) or dispositional (lying dormant to be activated under the appropriate circumstances): "our dispositional aliefs depend on the associational patterns than have been laid down in our minds as the result of our experiences and those of our genetic ancestors" (ibid.: 651). In this sense, alief is an automatic and arational response to particular stimuli. Yet just as humans possess associational patterns concerning heights, bed pans, dog faeces, and vomit that produce automatic affects and behaviours which contradict firmly held beliefs, it seems likely to me that humans also have associational patterns concerning god(s), spirits, and invisible forces that produce automatic affects and behaviours that contradict consciously held disenchanted beliefs.

In-Between Belief

Eric Schwitzgebel (b. 1962), an American philosopher who focuses on the philosophy of mind and the nature of belief, argues there are situations in which it is inappropriate to either ascribe or deny belief. Schwitzgebel describes the case of an imaginary professor named Juliet who firmly believes that all races are of equal intelligence and yet who remains overtly biased against the black students in her courses. Although Juliet "is prepared to argue coherently, sincerely, and vehemently for equality of intelligence", Juliet is nevertheless "systematically racist in most of her spontaneous reactions" (Schwitzgebel 2010: 532). In this example, the professor believes one thing and yet behaves as if she believed something else entirely.

Schwitzgebel favours a dispositional account of belief in which believing a given proposition means being disposed to act and react as if that proposition were the case. From the perspective of a narrow dispositional account of belief, the professor's failure to be disposed to act as if all races are of equal intelligence would seem to indicate that she lacks this particular belief. Yet Schwitzgebel argues for a broad and multidimensional dispositional account of belief: "… there must be cases in which the relevant dispositional structure is only partly possessed. There must, indeed, be something like a continuum, between full possession of all the relevant dispositions and possession of none of them …" (ibid.: 534).

According to Schwitzgebel, simply ascribing belief or disbelief in cases such as the one described above is overly simplistic. Instead, he argues that providing a thorough account of a person's complex dispositional structure is more useful. Juliet has, in some respects, the appropriate dispositional structure to ascribe belief as "she is disposed to judge or affirm, in good faith, both inwardly and outwardly, that all the races are intellectually equal…" and yet in other key respects "she lacks an egalitarian dispositional structure… in many of her emotional reactions and spontaneous intuitive judgments" (ibid.: 537). For Schwitzgebel, in such a case, saying either that Juliet believes or does not believe is insufficient. Instead, it would be necessary to explain when and in which circumstances Juliet is disposed toward egalitarian beliefs and when she is disposed instead toward racist ones. As Schwitzgebel puts it, in cases like Juliet's, "a simple answer won't do" (ibid.).

Schwitzgebel challenges Gendler's view that a person might believe one thing while alieving another. According to Schwitzgebel, Gendler's distinction between rational belief (the "vomit" is only rubber) and arational alief (disgust and reluctance) mischaracterizes both rational belief and automatic responses. He argues that automatic responses do change in the face of contradictory evidence or, in other words, that they are more reality-sensitive than Gendler admits. Considering Juliet, Schwitzgebel argues that she would have to be extraordinarily inflexible if her racist disposition remained intact even after sufficient exposure to very smart black students. To put this another way, it seems likely that after spending sufficient time with vomit-shaped rubber, my reluctance to put it in my mouth would eventually decrease. Importantly, Schwitzgebel also argues that our rational beliefs about the world are not always developed primarily in response to objective evidence. In other words, our rational beliefs are, according to this view, more reality-insensitive than Gendler proposes. He argues that Juliet's disposition to judge that races are intellectually equal is a product of her overall politics and liberal values and are thus unlikely to easily change: "[m]any liberals ... would be very slow to change their judgments about the intellectual equality of the races were good evidence of Caucasian superiority to start coming in" (ibid.: 540).

Schwitzgebel's account of in-between belief sheds light on the case of Amélie described above. For him, the problem would not be that Amélie believes the statue is purely symbolic and yet acts as though it may be efficacious. Instead, the problem lies with my desire to ascribe either belief or disbelief when such an ascription is overly simplistic. Schwitzgebel's argument that our rational beliefs are products of larger overarching ideals (e.g. liberalism) and are therefore reality-insensitive may also explain Amélie's reluctance to believe her fertility statue may be effective even when her actions and dispositions indicate some level of belief in its efficacy. Amélie's position as an educated college professor and her commitments to atheism are likely important contributing factors to her firmly held belief that the statue is purely symbolic. Likewise, the idea of disenchantment itself may be an important contributing factor in the disavowal of sincere belief in magic, spirits, and invisible forces more broadly.

Irony

Enchanted beliefs in magic, spirits, and invisible forces are increasingly difficult to maintain in modernity – not because the world or its inhabitants are actually disenchanted, but rather because *the idea* that the world is disenchanted is immensely influential both within and outside of the academy. The notion that humans have triumphantly overcome childish, misguided, and irrational superstitions is a central feature in accounts of modernity and in narratives of modernization. I suspect this notion has important consequences not only for what modern humans believe or half-believe but also for how they express or frame these beliefs or half-beliefs. Social pressure to disavow magical or superstitious beliefs and practices generate what I see as a uniquely modern variety of ironic fluid enchantment.

As I argued in Chapter 3, modern individuals face significant pressure both to overcome their own apparently deluded beliefs concerning magic or spirits and to actively disenchant the beliefs of others. For it is precisely by characterizing and excluding others as foolishly enchanted that we are able to imagine ourselves as advanced, rational, intelligent, and modern. Paradoxically, the allure of disenchantment is what drives recent descriptions of rational re-enchantment that I explored in Chapter 4. In order to maintain the "theoretical superiority" and "practical maturity" that disenchantment provides, accounts of rational re-enchantment either focus on the presence of enchanted delight without any associated deluded beliefs or else omit belief entirely and redefine enchantment as uniquely involving affective states (De Vriese 2010: 423). Outside of specific neo-pagan or New Age communities, believing in magic is a difficult position either to maintain or to defend since, as Keith Thomas claims, "astrology, witchcraft, magical healing, divination, ancient prophesies, ghosts and fairies are now all rightly disdained by intelligent persons ..." (Thomas 1971: ix).

Whether or not the disenchantment thesis provides an accurate account of historical developments, the *discourse* of disenchantment sets limits on the kinds of beliefs and practices that individuals are willing publicly to admit entertaining or engaging in. As the psychologist Stuart A. Vyse notes in his book *Believing in Magic: The Psychology of Superstition*, "many believers are reluctant to confess their superstitions for fear of ridicule" (Vyse 1997: 14). As a result, modern engagement with various enchanted ideas and practices is sometimes described with a certain ironic detachment. In a recent article on the topic of irony, Matt Dinan describes the "wry tone" of contemporary online horoscopes and recounts an episode in which one his students described his interest in astrology as "mostly ironic" (Dinan 2019: 133). For Dinan, ironically engaging in astrology permitted the student to maintain "a certain plausible deniability" concerning his interests (ibid.). The detachment or plausible deniability that irony provides allows those who ironically engage in various enchantments to experience the world as enchanted, while nevertheless adhering to the regulatory ideal that the discourse of disenchantment provides. As was the case with half-belief, alief, and in-between belief described above, ironic engagement with enchanted beliefs and practices constitutes a fuzzy middle-ground between outright belief or disbelief. A person who ironically engages with astrology, magic, or spirits behaves in ways that appear to be both enchanted *and* disenchanted at the same time. Once again, a clear binary distinction between belief and disbelief seems to be ineffective in such cases. Viewing enchantment instead as a broad spectrum of fluid and potentially contradictory beliefs and behaviours makes space for forms of modern enchantment that are influenced not only by a reluctance to admit sincere belief in the face of disenchantment but also by the "pervasively ironic bearing" of modern society (ibid.).

Play

Many of the enchantments that I have described in this book have been and continue to be taken very seriously. Accusations of witchcraft carried serious and often life-threatening consequences in premodernity. Likewise, when "baby witches" or newcomers to neo-pagan practice claimed to have hexed the moon in 2020, this produced serious outrage among some neo-pagans. Yet just as framing enchantment in terms of consistent firmly held belief ignores partial or in-between beliefs and ironic engagement with enchantment, viewing enchanted beliefs and practices as uniquely serious ignores those who playfully engage with magic, spirits, and invisible forces.

While play is sometimes viewed as mere frivolity or entertainment, according to Johan Huizinga, play is a central and unavoidable feature of both human life and civilization (Huizinga 1955). For Huizinga, play is "a well-defined quality of action which is different from 'ordinary' life" (ibid.: 4). This distinction between play and ordinary life is precisely what makes play a helpful concept for describing fluid enchantment. From the perspective of disenchanted modernity, rational and scientific explanations govern ordinary life. Enchantment disrupts this picture of a rule-governed and sterile modernity, as it involves recognizing and engaging with "the extraordinary that lives amid the familiar and everyday" (Bennett 2001: 4). Huizinga makes direct connections between play and enchantment; he argues that play "casts a spell over us" and "is enchanting" and describes the reassertion of ordinary life as a "collapse of the play spirit ... a disenchantment" (Huizinga 1955: 10, 21). For Huizinga, play involves a mix of belief and unbelief, exists on the borderline between a half-joking attitude and earnestness, and depends upon a fluid movement between serious-ness and the recognition that play is "only pretending" (ibid.: 139, 5, 8).

According to Huizinga, the otherworldly dimension of play is also present in ritual action. As he puts it, "the ritual act has all the formal and essential characteristics of play... particularly in so far as it transports the participants to another world" (ibid.: 18). Adam B. Seligman also connects play and ritual, noting that "playfulness is somehow inherent in ritual" and that both play and ritual create spaces in which humans "create, experience, and share alternative realities and orders" (Seligman et al. 2008: 70, 73). Seligman contrasts the playful mode inherent in ritual with what he refers to as the sin-cere mode, which privileges "a genuine and thoughtful state of inter-nal conviction", "self-examination", and "authenticity" (Seligman 2009: 1079). Whereas the playful ritual mode creatives a subjunctive "what-if" or "could-be" attitude, sincerity projects an "as is" attitude and creates a "totalistic, unambiguous vision of reality 'as it *really* is'" (Seligman et al. 2008: 7–8). Seligman associates the sincere "as is" mode with specific modern developments, including individualism, the Protestant Reformation, the Enlightenment, secular conscious-ness, and science – developments that are all typically associated with disenchantment (Seligman 2009). Although Seligman notes that both the playful and sincere modes for framing experience, action, and understanding co-exist in all societies, he argues in modernity, the sincere (or disenchanted) mode has become the "default posi-tion" (Seligman et al. 2008: 7).

If Seligman is correct in claiming that disenchanted modernity is characterized by a sincere "as is" mode of framing existence that relies on firmly held rational beliefs and internal convictions, it should come as no surprise that playfulness is often criticized as insincere and inauthentic. In their research on contemporary neo-pagans, Angela Coco and Ian Woodward describe distinctions within neo-paganism between authentic and serious practitioners and inexperienced neo-pagans who are often described as "baby witches" or "fluffy bunnies" (Coco and Woodward 2007). Neo-pagans who view themselves as both sincere and authentic often criticize newcomers to neo-paganism for being overly consumeristic, insufficiently serious, and inappropriately playful (ibid.). Younger witches who purchase spell kits sold in bookstores are sometimes accused of merely dabbling in witchcraft rather than seriously engaging with its principles and philosophy (ibid.: 493). Yet from the perspective of fluid enchantment, it would be a mistake to describe individuals who purchase commercially available spell kits and who playfully engage with magic, spirits, and invisible forces as disenchanted. As in the case of Amélie described above, something else is going on here. As it was with half-belief and irony, individuals who playfully engage with enchanted beliefs and practices and who frame existence using a playful subjunctive "what-if" mode resist the neat binary distinction between enchantment and disenchantment. From the perspective of fluid enchantment, such individuals are neither enchanted nor disenchanted; instead, they fluidly move between these two positions.

Conclusion

In this chapter, I argued that the various descriptions of enchantment, disenchantment, and re-enchantment that I outlined in previous chapters ignore the ways in which some contemporary individuals half-believe in and ironically or playfully engage with various enchantments. I outlined what I take to be a problematic and overly simplistic binary model of belief that is implicit in most theoretical approaches to enchantment, disenchantment, and re-enchantment and described three philosophical approaches to belief that highlight how beliefs are often partial, fluid, or "in-between". I argued that, rather than view enchantment and disenchantment in terms of a neat binary between two coherent sets of belief or consistent practices, it is more productive is to view modern enchantment as a spectrum that exists between the two poles of outright belief or disbelief in magic, spirits, and invisible forces. To describe this "in-between" state, I proposed a new term: "fluid enchantment". I also argued that social pressure to disavow enchanted or superstitious beliefs and practices create a uniquely modern form of ironic enchantment in which individuals engage with various enchantments while nevertheless maintaining their commitments to modern rationality. Finally, drawing from theoretical work on ritual and play, I described enchantment as involving a playful "what-if" attitude, a characterization that I explore more fully in the concluding chapter.

From the perspective of partial belief and fluid enchantment, questions as to whether the world was enchanted, whether it became disenchanted, and whether it has now become re-enchanted are unhelpful at best. For if *individual* belief and practice are too complex to be encapsulated by any simple binary formulation, it seems unlikely that any such binary can be productively used to describe *the world*. While, as I argued in Chapter 2, it seems impossible to know for certain the extent to which premodern humans straightforwardly and firmly believed in magic, spirits, and invisible forces, I suspect that even in this context the simple ascription of enchantment or disenchantment is problematic. More likely is that, as is the case today, premodern humans also oscillated between states of relative enchantment or disenchantment and that this oscillation depended upon many different contextual factors. Thus, while it seems clear to me that *some* people wholly accept enchanted beliefs and practices while *some* wholly reject these, it seems equally clear that *most* people fall instead somewhere between these two extremes.

An important corollary of this view is that it is possible to consider the extent to which any given individual or context is enchanted (i.e. the extent to which belief in and engagement with magic, spirits, and invisible forces is operative) as a *matter of degree* rather than as a simple matter of fact (enchanted or disenchanted). As Schwitzgebel argues in terms of belief, I suspect that when it comes to enchantment, a simple yes or no answer won't do. Instead, I suggest it is more productive to consider why, to what extent, and in which situations enchantment occurs rather than attempt to determine whether or not an individual is or is not enchanted. Also, if enchantment does include the "in-between" cases that I described, it also seems clear that, despite the prevalence and influence of the disenchantment narrative, modernity has neither expelled enchanted beliefs or practices, nor has it drained the world of meaning and significance. Instead, modernity and the disenchantment narrative in particular provide a discursive register that privileges rational and scientific explanations, or what Seligman refers to as a sincere "as is" mode of framing experience, action, and understanding. As I explain in the concluding chapter, there may be good reasons for resisting this mode of experiencing the world and for recognizing the fluid play of enchantment in modernity.

Conclusion

The Future of Enchantment

Enchantment is not just about ghosts, gods, and goodness ... It is also about wonder and delight.

Lori Beaman, *Reclaiming Enchantment*

No world comes without its otherwise.

Martin Savransky, *Around the Day in Eighty Worlds*

I would like to end this critical primer with some final thoughts on how the concept enchantment might best be deployed in future scholarship. As I explained in the Introduction, the term enchantment most often describes the implied negative space created by the apparent event or process of modern disenchantment. Seen through the lens of the disenchantment theses put forward by Max Weber, Marcel Gauchet, and Charles Taylor, enchantment typically denotes a collection of beliefs and practices that modern humans have triumphantly overcome, as well as a range of affective states to which modern disenchanted humans no longer have access. Yet, as the epigraph to this chapter suggests, scholars have attempted to re-imagine or "reclaim" enchantment by stripping the term of its earlier associations with "ghosts, gods, and goodness" (Beaman 2021: 4).

Examples of such scholarly efforts to reimagine enchantment include Michael Saler's arguments for delight without delusion, Jane Bennett's attempts to separate enchantment's affective states from supernatural sources, and more recently, Lori Beaman's attempt to distinguish enchantment from religion and the divine (Saler 2006; Bennett 2001; Beaman 2021). In this final chapter, I consider these attempts to reconfigure enchantment and argue that this reconfiguration risks dulling the promise and potential that enchantment holds when it is conceived instead as modernity's foil or constitutive *other*.

Reclaiming Enchantment

As I argued in Chapter 4, both Saler and Bennett reconfigure enchantment in important ways. In his description of re-enchantment, Saler describes enchantment as an experience that offers "fully secularized subjects an affirmation of existence" that is free from the "naïveté, irrationalism, or hypocrisy" associated with religion, superstition, and magic (Landy and Saler 2009: 2). In her description of the enchantment of modern life, Bennett describes enchantment as a mood of "fullness, plenitude, or liveliness" that is distinct from traditional theology, New Age religion, magic, and the supernatural (Bennett 2001: 5, 10–11, 8). In both cases, enchantment is reimagined primarily in terms of affective states and is viewed as wholly separate from posited supernatural entities or forces. Drawing on both Saler and Bennett, the Canadian religious studies scholar Lori Beaman (b. 1963) puts forward what is, to date, the most well-developed and convincing argument in favour of reconfiguring enchantment.

Beaman takes issue with the fact that enchantment has typically been imagined both in scholarship and more generally as a product of religion, magic, and the transcendent. More specifically, she rejects the "dominant position" that views enchantment as a product of religion or the divine (Beaman 2021: 3). Like Bennett and Saler, Beaman argues both that enchantment should primarily be associated with wonder and delight rather than with god(s) or ghosts and also that enchantment can be produced by nonreligious sources. As Beaman puts it, "[e]nchantment is not owned by religion. Wonder and delight belong to everyone ..." (ibid.: 6). Her project to reclaim enchantment as a conceptual tool for describing nonreligious sources and experiences of wonder and delight depends, therefore, upon a theoretical distinction between religion, magic, spirituality, and enchantment. In order to recognize nonreligious sources and experiences of enchantment, Beaman proposes "shedding the baggage of magic and religion and relocating the occurrence of enchantment as a possibility linked to multiple frequencies or registers" (ibid.: 5). She is particularly interested in natural sources of wonder and delight. For her, whereas experiences of enchantment produced by the natural world are capable of producing a revised ethics that can address the deeply damaging relationship between humans, the planet, and other non-human beings, equating religion with enchantment "has exacerbated the paucity of creative and strong responses to an impoverished relationship between humans and nature" (ibid.: 10). Beaman's project to reconfigure or reclaim enchantment is thus motivated by both theoretical and ecological concerns.

Like Bennett, Beaman rejects the disenchantment thesis, arguing that disenchantment is a myth. For Beaman, disenchantment describes a "theoretical concoction rather than an empirical reality" (ibid.: 4). In contrast to disenchantment, she describes enchantment both as a conceptual tool used by academics and as a feature of empirical reality or as "something that is experienced by people in day-to-day life in particular circumstances" (Beaman 2021: 2). I take issue with this distinction. It remains unclear to me why disenchantment is merely theoretical, while enchantment is somehow actual. Although humans certainly react in various ways to features of empirical reality and subsequently describe these reactions using specific terms, *enchantment itself* is not a feature of empirical reality. Instead, humans classify their subjective experiences using particular terms such as wonder, delight, or enchantment. While the links humans make between raw experience and concepts like enchantment may be consistent, they are nevertheless essentially arbitrary; the experiences or ideas that I classify with "enchantment" might equally be classified in different ways. Jonathan Z. Smith famously described "religion" as a scholarly construct, but his insights concerning the term religion are equally applicable to "enchantment". As Smith might put it,

> while there is a staggering amount of data, phenomena, of human experiences and expressions that might be characterized in one culture or another, by one criterion or another, as [enchantment] – there is no data for [enchantment]. [Enchantment] is solely the creation of the scholar's study. It is created for the scholar's analytic purposes by his [sic] imaginative acts of comparison and generalization.
>
> (Smith 1998: xi)

In support of her argument that disenchantment is merely a theoretical concoction, Beaman refers to the supposed persistence of enchantment in modernity. According to her, despite scholarly descriptions of the world as disenchanted, "enchantment, both immanent and transcendent, always remained active, even if unseen and ignored by scholars" (Beaman 2021: 4). Yet if concepts like enchantment are merely tools employed by scholars to describe certain features of the world, scholars were not ignoring enchantment, nor were they unable to *see* enchantment; instead, they were simply unwilling to *describe* the world or its features with that term.

I resist on both practical and theoretical grounds efforts to reconfigure the academic term "enchantment" such that it uniquely signifies wonder and delight and excludes beliefs (or half-beliefs) associated with ghosts, spirits, and invisible forces. From a practical standpoint, if the goal is to describe feelings of wonder and delight with a term that is free from the "baggage" of magic and religion, I suggest that it may be preferable to choose a term that is *already free* from these connotations such as "wonder" or "delight". From a theoretical standpoint, I argue that ignoring the ways "enchantment" has been associated with specific supernatural beliefs and practices impoverishes our ability to accurately describe the fate of magical beliefs and practices in modernity. Rather than view associations between enchantment and magic as baggage to be discarded, I take these associations to be precisely what makes "enchantment" such a useful term in the scholarly lexicon.

Academic terms are flexible. Indeed, my primary goal in this book has been to chart how "enchantment", "disenchantment", and "re-enchantment" have been deployed in different ways, by different scholars, and for different purposes. I am not, therefore, reluctant to discard associations between enchantment and magic because of a belief that enchantment possesses an essential core that would somehow be lost or damaged were it associated uniquely with wonder and delight. The issue, as Beaman suggests, is that concepts are consequential. Beaman aptly explores the notion that conceptual frameworks entail real-world consequences. For instance, she argues that reimagining enchantment as signifying wonder and delight while freeing the term of its religious baggage will permit "an enlarged enchantment-propelled ethics [that] has the potential to recraft human relationships with 'others'" (ibid.: 9). Likewise, although Beaman describes the concept of disenchantment as a myth that lacks any empirical reality, she nevertheless argues that discarding this myth is important not only for academic clarity but also for the beneficial real-world consequences this will produce. Yet in my view, denying disenchantment's empirical reality and equating enchantment with wonder ignores the ways the disenchantment narrative has shaped and continues to shape our interactions with other humans and the world. While belief in spirits and invisible forces seems prevalent in modernity, the notion that the world has become disenchanted continues to shape contemporary discourse, along with the ways modern subjects frame and express their own beliefs and practices.

The Promise of Enchantment

Although the word enchantment is not new, the academic concept enchantment as it is used in scholarship is inextricably linked with modernity. As I argued above, while things could certainly be otherwise, "enchantment" is typically understood as signifying the negative space created by the disenchantment thesis. Thus the concept "disenchantment", as it is used in scholarship, is itself a modern creation. Although enchantment is a modern concept, it is most often used to describe *nonmodern* beliefs, practices, and experiences. As I argued in Chapter 3, while the term enchantment is typically used to describe premodern belief in god(s), ghosts, and spirits, it is also used with reference to beliefs and practices that, while present in modernity, are nevertheless viewed as antithetical to specific modern values such as scientific rationality.

The Iron Cage of Disenchanted Discourse

Insofar as disenchantment denotes a shift from magical explanations to scientific ones, it seems clear that a variety of disenchantment has certainly taken place. Although the modern world may not have become disenchanted, modern *discourse* has. As Judith Butler notes, discourse involves institutionalized ways of thinking that set limits both on both acceptable speech and on acceptable conceptions of reality (Butler 1999). While discussions of magical powers and invisible forces may be deemed acceptable within some neo-pagan and New Age communities, public admissions of belief in magic or ghosts are nevertheless commonly deemed inappropriate. As the legal scholar Steven D. Smith claims, this reluctance to publicly admit supernatural conceptions of the world constitutes the disenchantment of secular discourse (Smith 2010).

Smith links the disenchantment of secular discourse with John Rawls's notion of public reason. For Rawls, given a plurality of dissenting views concerning "ultimate" questions such as the will of God, humans are unlikely to ever converge on a unified answer. As a result, when reasoning in public, Rawls argues that citizens must bracket and refrain from invoking "comprehensive doctrines" (e.g. religious views) and instead rely on reasons and justifications about which there is some consensus (ibid.: 14–17). Practically, this might involve framing an argument against eating meat in terms of animals' ability to feel pain rather than, for instance, in terms of Buddhist arguments in favour of vegetarianism. Smith argues that the disenchantment of secular discourse carries negative consequences. Because individuals often rely on supernatural conceptions of the world in framing important commitments, they must "smuggle" these commitments into public debates disguised in secular terms. Although Smith is primarily concerned with supernatural conceptions of the world that tend to be labelled "religious", supernatural conceptions that tend instead to be labelled "magical" are equally excluded from public discourse. The problem, for Smith, is that these limits on public speech create a "barren, unsatisfying, and shallow" public discourse and also make it difficult, if not impossible, for individuals to articulate their beliefs and priorities both to others or even to themselves (ibid.: 39).

Like Eric Schwitzgebel, whose approach to belief I explored in the preceding chapter, Smith favours a dispositional account of belief. For him, belief is more complicated than merely assenting to or denying a given proposition. Determining what we *really* believe involves both introspection and also a process of "reading ourselves" as a whole – a process that Smith argues must be cooperative (ibid.: 195–197).

Yet the disenchantment of contemporary discourse complicates any effort to productively and cooperatively explore our own beliefs or the beliefs of others. The result, for Smith, is a discursive iron cage:

> public discourse is impoverished because the constraints of secular rationalism prevent us from openly presenting, examining, and debating the sources and substance of our most fundamental normative commitments. Unable to acknowledge its deeper, determining strata, our discourse is condemned to superficiality.
>
> (Smith 2010: 211)

Smith suspects that despite the discursive limits that scientific rationality places on acceptable speech and acceptable conceptions of reality, most people believe there is more to reality than narratives of disenchantment suppose – even if they are often unwilling to discuss this openly or to imagine any reality beyond naturalistic scientific accounts.

The Wonder of Enchantment

Dismissing disenchantment as Beaman and others recommend risks ignoring the social (but no less empirical) discursive reality that disenchantment creates. But the theoretical reconfiguration proposed by Beaman and others also risks removing what is, in my view, an important conceptual tool for speaking about, thinking about, and playing with beliefs concerning posited supernatural entities and forces. According to my own cost-benefit analysis, we have more to gain by maintaining enchantment's dual nature and understanding enchantment to involve *both* significant affective states *and* magical or supernatural beliefs.

Unlike "religion", the term enchantment can be productively used to refer to a wide range of beliefs and practices that fall outside the confines of any particular religious belief system. The beliefs and practices that typically earn the designation "enchanted" (e.g. magic, "superstitions") have never been the exclusive territory of religious individuals. Indeed, most often religion has, in various ways and for various reasons, been defined in contradistinction to magic and superstition. But while "enchantment" is sometimes used as a near

synonym for superstition, it does not carry the same negative connotations of delusion or gullibility that "superstition" does. Instead, it
is commonly associated with positive affective states such as wonder
and delight. If enchantment's dual signification of both magic and
delight is maintained, scholars will not only retain a helpful descriptor in their lexicon but also may be encouraged to ask what, after
all, is so delightful or wonderful about magic and superstition in the
first place?

My tentative answer to this question relies on enchantment's position as modernity's constitutive *other*. Since Max Weber first articu-
lated the disenchantment thesis over a century ago, enchantment has
been an enduring foil to modernity. In contrasting modern scientific
rationality with premodern enchantment, generations of scholars
have emphasized and thereby enhanced the sincere "as-is" mode
of interpretation on which modern scientific rationality depends.
Although modernity has been amply criticized for its alienating
effects, both modernity and its effects are often imagined to be *inevitable*. Faced with scientific rationality's immense explanatory powers,
its growing status as *the only* means for explaining the world, and its
associated social value, a return to premodern enchantment is not
simply undesirable, but in fact impossible. For who could willingly
abandon reality *as it really is* in favour of what must now, in the harsh
light of disenchantment, be conceived as mere fantasy?

But fantasy is not always mere fantasy. As Adam B. Seligman argues,
while modernity has certainly privileged the sincere "as-is" mode, it
seems unlikely that the more playful subjunctive "what-if" mode of
experiencing and interpreting reality will ever disappear completely
(Seligman et al. 2008). Seen through the lens of fluid enchantment,
enchantment provides modern subjects with opportunities to play
with their ideas about reality, to resist final answers, and to fantasize
about other possible ways of being and belonging. In other words,
enchantment, like fantasy, can be productive. As Judith Butler puts it,

> The critical promise of fantasy, when and where it exists, is to chal-
> lenge the contingent limits of what will and will not be called reality.
> Fantasy is what allows us to imagine ourselves and others otherwise;
> it establishes the possible in excess of the real, it points elsewhere …
> (Butler 2004: 29)

Understood as involving fluid and playful engagement, enchantment not only produces wonder but also provides a productive space for *wondering* about how things could be otherwise.

Martin Savransky explores the pleasure and promise of thinking and experiencing things to be otherwise in his book *Around the Day in Eighty Worlds: Politics of the Pluriverse*. Savransky traces the links between scientific rationality and what he describes as a reductive and destructive "monification" of the world according to which only one possible configuration of reality is presumed to exist. According to Savransky, this monification of the world involves,

> the disqualification and devastation of difference brought about through capitalist supply chains and corrosive forms of laughter, through rational knowledges and colonial expansions, through development programs and socio-ecological plundering.
>
> (Savransky 2021: 5)

For Savransky, the modern rational scientific preference for unified and total explanations – what Seligman would refer to as the sincere "as-is" mode – is wielded as a "weapon of mass disqualification that creates and polices the border of what may count as real and what is dismissed as illusory, fantastical, superstitious, magical, or whimsical ..." (ibid.: 9). Yet Savransky argues the view there is exactly one true and complete description of the way the world is – what he calls realism – is an arbitrary decree rather than a theory or intellectual position (ibid.: 17).

Drawing on the work of the American philosopher and psychologist William James (1842–1910), Savransky argues for a *pluralistic* realism that takes seriously the possibility that realities which diverge from scientific rationality are not merely competing worldviews or interpretations but are *actually real*. Rather than accept a single reductive rational scientific explanation of the universe and everything in it, Savransky argues instead for an appreciation of the *pluriverse*: of multiple possible and actual configurations of reality. For Savransky, pluralistic realism is more than an intellectual position – it is political act:

> to subjunctively present alternatives to declarations about what "is" or imperatives about what "should be" is itself a political act – a radical one, to the degree that it breaks free of the glib relativism of merely reporting on alternative possibilities ("worldviews" etc.), and proceeds boldly to lend the "otherwise" full ontological weight so as to render it *viable as a real alternative*.
>
> (Savransky 2021: 43, italics in original).

Seen through the lens of pluralistic realism, the promise of fluid enchantment may also reside in its capacity for producing (or permitting) the experience of living in a world in which multiple realities overlap. Like fantasy and the subjunctive "what-if" modality, enchantment produces a productive space for thinking about, believing in, experiencing, and playing with other realities. We may not find solutions to the pressing existential threats that we face in the twenty-first century in our horoscopes, by interacting with spirits, or by casting magic spells. But to the extent that facing these threats requires us to imagine other ways of living in the world and with each other, enchantment may yet serve an important and perhaps indispensable social role.

The Future of "Enchantment"

Enchantment is a particularly ambiguous term since it can denote magical beliefs and practices, heightened emotional states that are free from superstitious delusion, or a complex combination of the two. As I have argued elsewhere, some of the problems with the concept enchantment that I have described in this book might be resolved if scholars who use the terms enchantment, disenchantment, and re-enchantment clearly explain what they mean by enchantment in the first place (Cuthbertson 2018b). Another strategy might involve scholars abandoning the term "enchantment" in favour of other terms, such as wonder, awe, or magic – especially if the goal is to re-imagine enchantment in ways that conceal or deny its long history as an academic concept. Using the distinction that I have proposed between spiritual and rational re-enchantment might also help to remove ambiguity in future scholarship.

Scholars may also wish to be more explicit about their own religious, non-religious, or metaphysical positions, along with their own political agendas. For instance, if Charles Taylor's argument that disenchanted modernity and its immanent frame results in a lack of fullness is to some extent a product of his own commitments to Catholicism, stating this explicitly might help his readers grasp not only his deployment of the term enchantment but also his larger goals and purpose. My own fascination with enchantment stems from its use as a marker of difference, as well as from my own uneasy self-identification as a superstitious atheist – as someone who is unwilling to believe that God or gods influence the course of human affairs but who nevertheless playfully believes at least some of the time that meaning may in fact exist outside of my own mind and thoughts.

It seems likely that enchantment will persist as a key concept for describing modernity, differentiating between magical and rational forms of thought, and for marking specific groups as insufficiently modern or rational. My hope is that by paying attention to enchantment's complex history, the various ways that the term has been used, and the specific agendas that it has supported, scholarship on this topic will continue to produce insights with greater transparency, precision, and clarity.

Further Reading

Disenchantment

Gauchet, Marcel. 1997. *The Disenchantment of the World: A Political History of Religion*. Translated by Oscar Burge. Princeton University Press.

Horkheimer, Max, Theodor Adorno. 2002. *The Dialectic of Enlightenment*. Translated by Edmund Jephcott. Stanford University Press.

Saler, Michael. 2006. "Modernity and Enchantment: A Historiographic Review". *The American Historical Review* 111.3: 692–716.

Taylor, Charles. 2007. *A Secular Age*. Harvard University Press.

Weber, Max. 2020. *Charisma and Disenchantment: The Vocation Lectures*. Translated by Damion Searls. New York Review of Books.

Pre-Modern Enchantment

Sahlins, Marshall. 2022. *The New Science of the Enchanted Universe: An Anthropology of Most of Humanity*. Princeton University Press.

Disenchantment as Modern Myth

Butler, Jon. 2010. "Disquieted History in A Secular Age". In Jonathan Vanantwerpen and Craig Calhoon (eds). *Varieties of Secularism in a Secular Age*. Harvard University Press.

Josephson-Storm, Jason Ā. 2017. *The Myth of Disenchantment: Magic, Modernity, and the Birth of the Human Sciences*. University of Chicago Press.

Robert A. Yelle and Lorenz Trein (eds). 2021 *Narratives of Disenchantment and Secularization: Critiquing Max Weber's Idea of Modernity*. Bloomsbury.

Enchantment and Exclusion

Dubuisson, Daniel. 2003. *The Western Construction of Religion: Myths, Knowledge, and Ideology*. Translated by William Sayers. John Hopkins University Press.

Styers, Randall. 2004. *Making Magic: Religion, Magic, and Science in the Modern World*. Oxford University Press.

Styers, Randall. 2017. "Bad Habits, Or How Superstition Disappeared in the Modern World". In Edward Bever and Randall Styers (eds). *Magic in the Modern World: Strategies of Repression and Legitimization*. Pennsylvania State University Press.

Re-enchantment

Bennett, Jane. 2001. *The Enchantment of Modern Life: Attachments, Crossings, and Ethics*. Princeton University Press.

Landy, Joshua and Michael Saler. 2009. *The Re-enchantment of the World: Secular Magic in a Rational Age*. Stanford University Press.

Partridge, Christopher. 2004. *The Re-enchantment of the West, Volume 1: Alternative Spiritualities, Sacralization, Popular Culture and Occulture*. T&T Clark.

Partridge, Christopher. 2005. *The Re-enchantment of the West, Volume 2: Studies in Sacralization and Occulture*. T&T Clark.

Saler, Michael. 2012. *As If: Modern Enchantment and the Literary Prehistory of Virtual Reality*. Oxford University Press.

References

Albanese, Catherine L. 1999. "The Subtle Energies of Spirit: Explorations in Metaphysical and New Age Spirituality". *Journal of the American Academy of Religion* 67.2: 305–325.

Albanese, Catherine L. 2000. "The Aura of Wellness: Subtle-Energy Healing and New Age Religion". *Religion and American Culture: A Journal of Interpretation* 10.1: 29–55.

Anonymous. 1890. "Concerning Negro Sorcery". *The Journal of American Folklore* 3.11: 281–287.

Arnal, William E. and Russell T. McCutcheon. 2013. *The Sacred is the Profane: The Political Nature of "Religion"*. Oxford University Press.

Asad, Talal. 2003. *Formations of the Secular: Christianity, Islam, Modernity*. Stanford University Press.

Aupers, Stef. 2009. "The Force is Great: Enchantment and Magic in Silicon Valley". *Masaryk University Journal of Law and Technology* 3.1: 153–174.

Aupers, Stef and Dick Houtman. 2005. "'Reality Sucks': On Alienation and Cybergnosis". *International Journal of Theology* 2005.1: 2–11.

Bailey, Lee Worth. 2005. *The Enchantments of Technology*. University of Illinois Press.

Bailey, Michael D. 2007. *Magic and Superstition in Europe: A Concise History from Antiquity to the Present*. Rowman & Littlefield.

Bailey, Michael D. 2013. *Fearful Spirits, Reasoned Follies: The Boundaries of Superstition in Late Medieval Europe*. Cornell University Press.

Battersby, Christine. 1981. "An Enquiry Concerning the Humean Woman". *Philosophy* 56.217: 303–312.

Beaman, Lori G. 2021. "Reclaiming Enchantment: The Transformational Possibilities of Immanence". *Secularism and Nonreligion* 10.8: 1–14. https://secularismandnonreligion.org/articles/10.5334/snr.149

Belk, Russell, Henri Weiko, and Robert V. Kozinets. 2021. "Enchantment and Perpetual Desire: Theorizing Disenchanted Enchantment and Technology Adoption". *Marketing Theory* 21.1: 25–51.

Bell, Matthew. 2014. *Melancholia: The Western Malady*. Cambridge University Press.

Bennett, Jane. 2001. *The Enchantment of Modern Life: Attachments, Crossings, and Ethics*. Princeton University Press.

Bennett, Jane. 2010. *Vibrant Matter: A Political Ecology of Things*. Duke University Press.

Berger, Helen A. 2019. *Solitary Pagans: Contemporary Witches, Wiccans, and Others who Practice Alone*. University of South Carolina Press.

Berger, Peter L. 1979. *The Heretical Imperative: Contemporary Possibilities of Religious Affirmation*. Anchor Books.

Berger, Peter L. 2012. "Further Thoughts on Religion and Modernity". *Society* 49.4: 313–316.

Bruce, Steve. 1997. "The Pervasive World-View: Religion in Pre-Modern Britain". *The British Journal of Sociology* 48.4: 667–680.

Bruce, Steve. 2002. *God is Dead: Secularization in the West*. Blackwell Publishers.

Bruce, Steve. 2011. *Secularization: In Defence of an Unfashionable Theory*. Oxford University Press.

Burnett, Cathy and Guy Merchant. 2018. "Affective Encounters: Enchantment and the Possibility of Reading for Pleasure". *Literacy* 52.2: 62–69.

Butler, Judith. 1999. *Gender Trouble: Feminism and the Subversion of Identity*. Routledge.

Butler, Judith. 2004. *Undoing Gender*. Routledge.

Butler, Jon. 2010. "Disquieted History in A Secular Age". In Jonathan Vanantwerpen and Craig Calhoon (eds). *Varieties of Secularism in a Secular Age*. Harvard University Press.

Cameron, Euan. 2010. *Enchanted Europe: Superstition, Reason, and Religion, 1250–1750*. Oxford University Press.

Casanova, José. 1994. *Public Religions in the Modern World*. University of Chicago Press.

Chakrabarty, Dipesh. 2002. *Habitations of Modernity: Essays in the Wake of Subaltern Studies*. University of Chicago Press.

Chaudhary, Mohammad Yaqub. 2019. "Augmented Reality, Artificial Intelligence, and the Re-enchantment of the World". *Zygon* 54.2: 454–478.

Clough, Patricia Ticineto and Jean Halley. 2007. *The Affective Turn: Theorizing the Social*. Duke University Press.

Coco, Angela and Ian Woodward. 2007. "Discourses of Authenticity Within a Pagan Community: The Emergence of the 'Fluffy Bunny' Sanction". *Journal of Contemporary Ethnography* 36.5: 479–504.

Conway, D.J. 1999. *Crystal Enchantments: A Complete Guide to Stones and Their Magical Properties*. Crossing Press.

Cook, Julia. 2016. "Young Adults' Hopes for the Long-Term Future: From Re-enchantment with Technology to Faith in Humanity". *Journal of Youth Studies* 19.4: 517–532.

Cooper, Michael T. 2009. "The Roles of Nature, Deities, and Ancestors in Constructing Religious Identity in Contemporary Druidry". *The Pomegranate* 11.1: 58–73.

Cox, David G. 2015. "'Half Bacchanalian, Half Devout': White Intellectuals, Black Folk Culture, and the 'Negro Problem'". *American Nineteenth Century History* 16.3: 241–267.

Cuthbertson, Ian Alexander. 2016. "Everyday Enchantments and Secular Magic in Montreal". PhD diss. Queen's University.

Cuthbertson, Ian Alexander. 2018a. "Preaching to the Choir? Religious Studies and Religionization". In Brad Stoddard (ed.). *Method Today: Redescribing Approaches to the Study of Religion*. Equinox.

Cuthbertson, Ian Alexander. 2018b. "The Problem of Enchantment". *Religion Compass* 12: e12285. https://doi.org/10.1111/rec3.12285

Darghawth, Rasha. 2013. "Contemporary Mediumship: Anthropological Perspectives on the Long Island Medium". *Totem* 21.1: 82–90.

Dawkins, Richard. 2006. *The God Delusion*. Black Swan.

Dawkins, Richard. 2011. *The Magic of Reality: How We Know What's Really True*. Simon & Schuster.

De Vriese, Herbert. 2010. "The Charm of Disenchantment: A Quest for the Intellectual Attraction of Secularization Theory". *Sophia* 49.3: 407–428.

Diabazar, P., C. Lindner, M. Meissner, and J. Naeff. 2013. "Questioning Urban Modernity". *European Journal of Cultural Studies* 34.4: 643–658.

Dinan, Matt. 2019. "Irony: What Does It Mean to Like Something Ironically". Retrieved from https://hedgehogreview.com/issues/reality-and-its-alternatives/articles/irony

Doyle, Arthur Conan. 1996. *The Case-book of Sherlock Holmes*. Oxford University Press.

Doyle White, Ethan. 2015. *Wicca: History, Belief, and Community in Modern Pagan Witchcraft*. Sussex Academic Press.

Drewry, M. Damaris J. 2003. "Purported After-Death Communication and its Role in the Recovery of Bereaved Individuals: A Phenomenological Study". *Proceedings (The Academic of Religion and Psychical Research)*, October: 74–87.

Dubuisson, Daniel. 2003. *The Western Construction of Religion: Myths, Knowledge, and Ideology*. Translated by William Sayers. John Hopkins University Press.

Dubuisson, Daniel. 2016. *Religion and Magic in Western Culture*. Translated by Martha Cunningham. Brill.

Durkheim, Émile. 1915. *The Elementary Forms of Religious Life*. Translated by Joseph Ward Swain. George Allen & Unwin.

Eire, Carlos M. N. 2016. *Reformations: The Early Modern World, 1450-1650*. Yale University Press.

Eisenstadt, S. N. 2000. "Multiple Modernities". *Daedalus* 129.1: 1–29.

Eneborg, Yusuf Muslim. 2014. "The Quest for 'Disenchantment' and the Modernization of Magic". *Islam and Christian-Muslim Relations* 25.4: 419–432.

Frazer, James George. 1940. *The Golden Bough: A Study in Magic and Religion*. Macmillan.

Gauchet, Marcel. 1997. *The Disenchantment of the World: A Political History of Religion*. Translated by Oscar Burge. Princeton University Press.

Gauchet, Marcel. 2004. *Un Monde Désenchanté?* Les Editions de L'Atelier.

Gaukroger, Stephen. 2005. "Science, Religion and Modernity". *Critical Quarterly* 4: 1–31.

Gecewicz, Claire. 2018. "'New Age' Beliefs Common among Both Religious and Nonreligious Americans". Retrieved from www.pewresearch. org/fact-tank/2018/10/01/new-age-beliefs-common-among-both-religious-and-nonreligious-americans/.

Gendler, Tamaer Szabó. 2008. "Alief and Belief". *The Journal of Philosophy* 105.10: 634–663.

Gibson, James William. 2009. *A Reenchanted World: The Quest for a New Kinship with Nature*. Macmillan.

Gibson, James William. 2010. "World of Wonder: Toward a Re-enchantment with Nature". *Earth Island Journal* 4: 56–60.

Giddens, Anthony and Phillip W. Sutton. 2021. *Essential Concepts in Sociology*. Polity Press.

Globe and Mail. 1887. *The Primitive Indians: Some Striking Characteristics of the Vanished Race. The Globe and Mail*, 29 October: 12.

Göle, Nilüfer. 2010. "The Civilizational, Spatial, and Sexual Powers of the Secular". In Michael Warner, Jonathan Vanantwerpen, and Craig Calhoon. (eds) *Varieties of Secularism in a Secular Age*. Harvard University Press.

Greyson, Lauren. 2019. *Vital Enchantments: Biophilia, Gaia, Cosmos, and the Affectively Ecological*. Punctum Books.

Gumbrecht, Hans Ulrich. 2009. "'Lost in Focused Intensity': Spectator Sports and Strategies of Re-Enchantment". In Landy Joshua and Michal Saler (eds). *The Re-enchantment of the World: Secular Magic in a Rational Age*. Stanford University Press.

Hanegraaff, Wouter J. 1996. *New Age Religion and Western Culture: Estotericism in the Mirror of Secular Thought*. Brill.

Hanegraaff, Wouter J. 2003. "How Magic Survived the Disenchantment of the World". *Religion* 33: 357–380.

Harris, Sam. 2005. *The End of Faith: Religion, Terror, and the Future of Reason*. W. W. Norton.

Harrison, Robert. 2009. "Homeless Gardens". In Landy Joshua and Michal Saler (eds). *The Re-Enchantment of the World: Secular Magic in a Rational Age*. Stanford University Press.

Helliwell, John F., Richard Layard, Jeffrey D. Sachs, and Jan-Emmanuel De Neve (eds). 2022. "World Happiness Report 2020". Retrieved from https://worldhappiness.report/ed/2020/.

Hoo, Misha. 2019. "Neopagan versus New Age Magic: Two Diverse Approaches to the Election of Trump". *International Journal of Religion and Spirituality in Society* 9.3: 33–44.

Horkheimer, Max, Theodor Adorno. 2002. *The Dialectic of Enlightenment* Translated by Edmund Jephcott. Stanford University Press.

Huizinga, Johan. 1955. *Homo Ludens: A Study of the Play Element in Culture*. The Beacon Press.

Hunter, Jennifer. 1998. *21st Century Wicca: A Young Witch's Guide to Living the Magical Life*. Citadel Press.

IARP. Undated a. "Learn about Reiki". Retrieved from https://iarp.org/learn-about-reiki/.

IARP. Undated b. "Reiki and the Chakras: A Gateway for Opening Spiritual Gifts". Retrieved from https://iarp.org/reiki-and-the-chakras-gateway-for-opening-spiritual-gifts/.

IPSOS. 2007. "Survey on Beliefs". Retrieved from www.ipsos.com/ipsos-mori/en-uk/survey-beliefs.

Jackson, Chris. 2019. "Divides Among Public Opinion on Astrology". Retrieved from www.ipsos.com/en-us/news-polls/astrology-horoscopes

Jackson, Chris. 2021. "Over a Third of Americans Believe in Ghosts and UFOs". Retrieved from www.ipsos.com/en-us/news-polls/belief-in-ghosts-2021

Jakobsen, Janet R. and Anne Pellegrini. 2008. *Secularisms*. Duke University Press.

Jones, Karen and Michael Zell. 2005. "'The Divels Speciall Instruments': Women and Witchcraft Before the 'Great Witch-Hunt'". *Social History* 30.1: 45–63.

Jorgensen, Danny L. and Scott E. Russell. 2000. "American Neopaganism: The Participants' Social Identities". *Journal for the Scientific Study of Religion* 38.3: 325–338.

Jortner, Adam. 2017. "Witches as Liars: Witchcraft and Civilization in the Early American Republic". In Edward Bever and Randall Styers (eds). *Magic in the Modern World: Strategies of Repression and Legitimization*. Pennsylvania State University Press.

Josephson-Storm, Jason Ā. 2006. "When Buddhism Became a 'Religion': Religion and Superstition in the Writings of Inoue Enryō". *Japanese Journal of Religious Studies* 33.1: 143–168.

Josephson-Storm, Jason Ā. 2017. *The Myth of Disenchantment: Magic, Modernity, and the Birth of the Human Sciences.* University of Chicago Press.

Josephson-Storm, Jason Ā. 2021. "Max Weber and the Rationalization of Magic". In Robert A. Yelle and Lorenz Trein (eds). *Narratives of Disenchantment and Secularization: Critiquing Max Weber's Idea of Modernity.* Bloomsbury.

Kalberg, Stephen. 1980. "Max Weber's Types of Rationality: Cornerstones for the Analysis of Rationalization Processes in History". *The American Journal of Sociology* 86.5: 1145–1179.

Kambhampaty, Anna P. 2021. "Many Americans Say They Believe in Ghosts. Do You?" *The New York Times*, 28 October. Retrieved from www.nytimes.com/2021/10/28/style/do-you-believe-in-ghosts.html.

Keurst, John Ter. 1939. "Comparative Differences Between Superstitious and Non-Superstitious Children". *The Journal of Experimental Education* 7.4: 261–267.

Kieckhefer, Richard. 2014. *Magic in the Middle Ages.* Cambridge University Press.

Kwilecki, Susan. 2009. "Twenty-First-Century American Ghosts: The After-Death Communication-Therapy and Revelation from Beyond the Grace". *Religion and American Culture: A Journal of Interpretation* 19.1: 101–133.

Landy, Joshua. 2009. "Modern Magic: Jean-Eugène Robert-Houdin and Stéphane Mallarmé". In Landy Joshua and Michal Saler (eds). *The Re-enchantment of the World: Secular Magic in a Rational Age.* Stanford University Press.

Landy, Joshua and Michael Saler. 2009. *The Re-enchantment of the World: Secular Magic in a Rational Age.* Stanford University Press.

Latour, Bruno. 1993. *We Have Never Been Modern.* Harvard University Press.

Lewis, James R. 1992. "Approaches to the Study of the New Age Movement". In Lewis, James R. and Melton J. Gordon (eds) *Perspectives on the New Age.* SUNY Press.

Maddrell, Avril. 2022. "'It Was Magical': Intersections of Pilgrimage, Nature, Gender and Enchantment as a Potential Bridge to Environmental Action in the Anthropocene". *Religions* 13.319: 1–20.

Mahmood, Saba. 2010. "Can Secularism Be Otherwise?" In Michael Warner, Jonathan Vanantwerpen, and Craig Calhoon (eds). *Varieties of Secularism in a Secular Age.* Harvard University Press.

Malinowski, Bronisław. 1954. *Magic, Science and Religion: And Other Essays.* Anchor Books.

Martin, Dale B. 2004. *Inventing Superstition: From the Hippocratics to the Christians*. Harvard University Press.

Martin, David. 2014. "Secularization: An International Debate from a British Perspective". *Society* 51.5: 464–471.

Masuzawa, Tomoko. 2005. *The Invention of World Religions*. University of Chicago Press.

Mauss, Marcel. 1950. *A General Theory of Magic*. Routledge and Kegan Paul.

Maxwell-Stuart, P. G. 2011. *Witch Beliefs and Witch Trials in the Middle Ages: Documents and Readings*. Continuum.

McCarthy, J. P. Wright, J. Wallace and Andy Dearden. 2005. "The Experience of Enchantment in Human-Computer Interaction". *Personal and Ubiquitous Computing* 10.6: 369–378.

McCutcheon, Russell T. 1997. *Manufacturing Religion: The Discourse on Sui Generis Religion and the Politics of Nostalgia*. Oxford University Press.

McLaughlin, Katy. 2016. "These Real-Life Ghostbusters Will Help Sell Your Haunted House". *The Wall Street Journal*, 27 October. Retrieved from www.wsj.com/articles/these-real-life-ghostbusters-will-help-sell-your-haunted-house-1477578503.

Moore, Rachel O. 2002. "Re-enchanted Enchantment: Watching Movies in the Movies". *Screens* 15.1/2: 161–176.

Moore, David W. 2005. "Three in Four Americans Believe in Paranormal". Retrieved from https://news.gallup.com/poll/16915/three-four-americans-believe-paranormal.aspx.

Musacchio, Jaqueline Marie. 2005. "Lambs, Coral, Teeth and the Intimate Intersection of Religion and Magic in Renaissance Tuscany". In Cornelison, Sally and Scott B. Montgomery (eds). *Images, Relics and Devotional Practices in Medieval and Renaissance Italy*. Arizona State University Press.

Nedopstup, Rebecca. 2009. *Superstitious Regimes: Religion and Politics of Chinese Modernity*. Harvard University Press.

New York Times. 1892. "Poor Subjects for Education: The Pueblo Indians Victims of the Darkest Superstition". *The New York Times*, 23 August.

New York Times. 1894. "Against Woman Suffrage: Her Enfranchisement Would Upset the Human Fabric". *The New York Times*, 7 May.

New York Times. 1909. "Witches and their Craft". *The New York Times*, 22 May.

OED. 1971. "Enchantment". *Oxford English Dictionary*. Oxford University Press.

Parkman, Francis. 1866. "Indian Superstitions". *American Eye*, July.

Partridge, Christopher. 2002. "The Disenchantment and Re-enchantment of the West: The Religio-Cultural Context of Contemporary Western Christianity". *The Evangelical Quarterly* 74.3. 235–256.

Partridge, Christopher. 2004. *The Re-enchantment of the West, Volume 1: Alternative Spiritualities, Sacralization, Popular Culture and Occulture.* T&T Clark.

Partridge, Christopher. 2005. *The Re-enchantment of the West, Volume 2: Studies in Sacralization and Occulture.* T&T Clark.

Pew. 2014. "Religion in Latin America: Widespread Change in a Historically Catholic Region". Pew Research Center. 13 November.

Pew. 2017. "Religious Belief and National Belonging in Central and Eastern Europe". Pew Research Center. 10 May.

Pew. 2018. "The Religious Typology". Pew Research Center. 29 August.

Pew. 2018a. "Being Christian in Western Europe". Pew Research Center. 29 May.

Pew. 2021. "Religion in India: Tolerance and Segregation". Pew Research Center. 29 June.

Pew. 2021a. "What Makes Life Meaningful? Views From 17 Advanced Economies". Pew Research Center. November 2021.

Pew. 2021b. "Few Americans Blame God or Say Faith Has Been Shaken Amid Pandemic, Other Tragedies". Pew Research Center, 23 November.

Piaget, Jean. 1973. *The Child's Conception of the World.* Paladin.

Pike, Sarah M. 2004. *New Age and Neopagan Religions in America.* Columbia University Press.

Prahlad, Anand. 2021 "Tearing Down Monuments: Missed Opportunities, Silences, and Absences – A Radical Look at Race in American Folklore Studies". *Journal of American Folklore* 134.533: 258–264.

Prezioso, M. G. 2021. "Enchantment and Understanding in Philip Pullman's *His Dark Materials*: Advancing Cognition Through Literature". *Children's Literature in Education* 52: 543–554.

Price, H. H. and R. B. Braithwaite. 1964. "Symposium: Half-Belief". *Proceedings of the Aristotelian Society, Supplementary Volumes* 38 (1964): 149–174.

Rayburn, Otto Ernest. 1959. "The 'Granny Woman' in the Ozarks". *Midwest Folklore* 9.3: 145–148.

Riordan, Suzanne. 1992. "Channeling: A New Revelation?" In Lewis, James R. and Melton J. Gordon (eds). *Perspectives on the New Age.* SUNY Press.

Roberts, John W. 2021. "Systemic Racism in American Folkloristics". *Journal of American Folklore* 134.533: 265–271.

Roper. 2005. "Paradise Polled: Americans and the Afterlife". Retrieved from https://ropercenter.cornell.edu/paradise-polled-americans-and-afterlife.

Ross, Steven David. 2012. *Enchanting: Beyond Disenchantment.* State University of New York Press.

Ryan, Phil. 2014. *After the New Atheist Debate.* University of Toronto Press.

Saler, Michael. 2006. "Modernity and Enchantment: A Historiographic Review". *The American Historical Review* 111.3: 692–716.

Saler, Michael. 2012. *As If: Modern Enchantment and the Literary Prehistory of Virtual Reality.* Oxford University Press.

Saler, Michael. 2021. "The Disenchanted Enchantments of the Modern Imagination and 'Fictionalism'". In Robert A. Yelle and Lorenz Trein (eds). *Narratives of Disenchantment and Secularization: Critiquing Max Weber's Idea of Modernity.* Bloomsbury.

Salmond, Noel. 2006. *Hindu Iconoclasts: Rammohun Roy, Dayananda Sarasvati, and Nineteenth-Century Polemics Against Idolatry.* Wilfred Laurier University Press.

Savranksy, Martin. 2021. *Around the Day in Eighty Worlds: Politics of the Pluriverse.* Duke University Press.

Schaeffer, Donovan O. 2015. *Religions Affects: Animality, Evolution, and Power.* Duke University Press.

Schultz, Karsten A. 2017. "Decolonizing Political Ecology: Ontology, Technology and 'Critical' Enchantment". *Journal of Political Ecology* 24: 124–143.

Schwitzgebel, Eric. 2010. "Acting Contrary to Our Professed Beliefs or the Gulf Between Occurrent Judgment and Dispositional Belief". *Pacific Philosophical Quarterly* 91: 531–553.

Scientific American. 1905. "Superstitions that Prevail in Rural Sections". *Scientific American* 92.21: 418–419.

Scribner, Robert W. 1993. "The Reformation, Popular Magic, and the 'Disenchantment of the World'". *The Journal of Interdisciplinary History* 23.3: 475–494.

Seligman, Adam B. 2009. "Ritual, the Self, and Sincerity". *Social Research* 76.4: 1073–1096.

Seligman, Adam B., Robert P. Weller, Michael Puett, and Bennett Simon. 2008. *Ritual and Its Consequences: An Essay on the Limits of Sincerity.* Oxford University Press.

Sideris, Lisa H. 2017. *Consecrating Science: Wonder, Knowledge, and the Natural World.* University of California Press.

Simmel, Georg. 1997. "The Metropolis and Mental Life". In David Frisby and Mike Featherstone (eds). *Simmel on Culture: Selected Writings.* Sage Publications.

Sizemore, Michelle. 2018. *American Enchantment: Rituals of the People in the Post-Revolutionary World.* Oxford University Press.

Skinner, B. F. 1948. "'Superstition' in the Pigeon". *Journal of Experimental Psychology* 38: 168–172.

Smith, J. Z. 1998. "Religion, Religions, Religious". In Mark C. Taylor (ed.). *Critical Terms for Religious Studies.* University of Chicago Press.

Smith, Steven D. 2010. *The Disenchantment of Secular Discourse*. Harvard University Press.

Stark, Rodney. 1999. "Secularization RIP". *Sociology of Religion* 60.3: 249–273.

Stone, Alison. 2006. "Adorno and the Disenchantment of Nature". *Philosophy & Social Criticism* 32.2: 231–253.

Styers, Randall. 2004. *Making Magic: Religion, Magic, and Science in the Modern World*. Oxford University Press.

Styers, Randall. 2017. "Bad Habits, Or How Superstition Disappeared in the Modern World". In Edward Bever and Randall Styers (eds). *Magic in the Modern World: Strategies of Repression and Legitimization*. Pennsylvania State University Press.

Szerszynski, Bronisław. 2005. *Nature, Technology and the Sacred*. Wiley.

Taylor, Charles. 1991. *The Malaise of Modernity*. Anansi.

Taylor, Charles. 2002. "Modern Social Imaginaries". *Public Culture* 14.1: 91–124.

Taylor, Charles. 2007. *A Secular Age*. Harvard University Press.

Taylor, Charles. 2010. "Afterword: Apologia Pro Libro Suo". In Jonathan Vanantwerpen and Craig Calhoon (eds). *Varieties of Secularism in a Secular Age*. Harvard University Press.

Theborn, Göran. 2003. "Entangled Modernities". *European Journal of Social Theory* 6.3: 293–305.

Thomas, Keith. 1971. *Religion and the Decline of Magic*. Scribner.

Torpey, John. 2012. "Religion and Secularization in the United States and Western Europe". In Philip Gorski, Davind Kyuman Kim, John Torpey, and Jonathan VanAntwerpen (eds). *the Post-Secular in Question; Religion in Contemporary Society*. NYU Press.

Tylor, Edward Burnett. 2010. *Primitive Culture: Researches into the Development of Mythology, Religion, Art, and Custom*. Cambridge University Press.

Urban, Hugh B. 2015. *New Age, Neopagan, and New Religious Movements: Alternative Spirituality in Contemporary America*. University of California Press.

Vyse, Stuart A. 1997. *Believing in Magic: The Psychology of Superstition*. Oxford University Press.

Wadler, Joyce. 2008. "Supernatural Cleaning Methods". *The New York Times*, 29 October. Retrieved from www.nytimes.com/2008/10/30/garden/30/haunted.html.

Wagner, Peter. 2012. *Modernity: Understanding the Present*. Polity.

Walker, William. 1990. "Locke Minding Women: Literary History, Gender, and the Essay". *Eighteenth-Century Studies* 23.3: 245–268.

Warner, Michael, Jonathan Vanantwerpen, Craig Calhoon, and Michael Warner. 2010. "Introduction" In Jonathan Vanantwerpen and Craig

Calhoon (eds). *Varieties of Secularism in a Secular Age*. Harvard University Press.

Weber, Max. 1958. *The Protestant Ethic and the Spirit of Capitalism*. Translated by Talcott Parsons. Charles Scribner and Sons.

Weber, Max. 1963. *The Sociology of Religion*. Translated by Ephraim Fischoff. Beacon Press.

Weber, Max. 2019. *Economy and Society*. Translated by Keith Tribe. Harvard University Press.

Weber, Max. 2020. *Charisma and Disenchantment: The Vocation Lectures*. Translated by Damion Searls. New York Review of Books.

Weigel, Jen. 2010. "How to Remove a Ghost". Retrieved from www.chicago tribune.com/lifestyles/ct-xpm-2010-10-22-ct-tribu-weigel-ghosts-20101022-story.html.

White, Cassandra. 2019. "Validation, Comfort, and Syncretic Belief in the Afterlife: US Viewers' Perceptions of *Long Island Medium*". *Anthropology of Consciousness* 30.1: 90–112.

Wilson, Bryan R. 1982. *Religion in Sociological Perspective*. Oxford University Press.

YouGov. 2022. "Daily Survey: Life and Society". 22–26 February. Retrieved from https://docs.cdn.yougov.com/70et3512ml/tabs_Life_and_Society_20220222.pdf

Zinnbauer, Brian J., Kenneth I. Pargament, Brenda Cole, Mark S. Rye, Eric M. Butler, Timothy G. Belavich, Kathleen M. Hipp, Allie B. Scott, Jill L. Kadar. 1997. "Religion and Spirituality: Unfuzzying the Fuzzy". *Journal for the Scientific Study of Religion* 36.4: 549–564.

Index

www.ingramcontent.com/pod-product-compliance
Lightning Source LLC
Chambersburg PA
CBHW051433270326
41935CB00018B/1818